The Independent Actor

The Independent Actor

An Accessible Companion for All Actors

SALLY ANN GRITTON

methuen | drama

LONDON • NEW YORK • OXFORD • NEW DELHI • SYDNEY

METHUEN DRAMA
Bloomsbury Publishing Plc
50 Bedford Square, London, WC1B 3DP, UK
1385 Broadway, New York, NY 10018, USA
29 Earlsfort Terrace, Dublin 2, Ireland

BLOOMSBURY, METHUEN DRAMA and the Methuen Drama logo are
trademarks of Bloomsbury Publishing Plc

First published in Great Britain 2024

For legal purposes the Acknowledgements on p. xvii constitute an
extension of this copyright page.

Cover design: Chris Bromley
Cover images: Woman (© faestock / AdobeStock);
Migratory birds (© SYI uncensored photo / AdobeStock)

A catalogue record for this book is available from the British Library.

ISBN: HB: 978-1-3502-7260-6
         PB: 978-1-3502-7261-3
       ePDF: 978-1-3502-7263-7
      eBook: 978-1-3502-7262-0

Typeset by Integra Software Services Pvt. Ltd.
Printed and bound in Great Britain

To find out more about our authors and books visit www.bloomsbury.com
and sign up for our newsletters.

Dedicated to Hatch, Joni and Malley

CONTENTS

THE AUTHOR

Sally Ann Gritton

MA PGCLTHE FHEA FRSA

Sally Ann Gritton is Principal and CEO of Mountview, a world-class drama school based in Peckham, South London. She attended Goldsmiths College and Kings College, University of London and RADA. Her freelance career as an actor and director led to her becoming Artistic Director of Sorted Productions. Here she championed emerging artists in Wales, platformed Welsh writing in London, toured work in England and Wales and produced a regular *Sorted Symposium: Welsh Writing in English* at Soho Theatre. She moved into the actor training sector some twenty years ago following her passion to support new artists. Specialising in developing forward thinking, collaborative models of training for actors, her graduates go on to gain roles in theatre, film, television and voice-recorded media work nationally and internationally, and work widely across the creative industries and beyond.

PREFACE

There are many ways to achieve an acting career. This book aims to demystify the concept of training for all actors at any stage in their development, taught or untaught. To those of you on the cusp of formal training, those creating their own bespoke learning path, to the mature student with life experience, those engaged in actor training and to untrained and curious *will*-be actors – gaining your skills can take a variety of routes.

There are many actors across the decades who did not train formally. The drive to achieve your goals can be led by your natural curiosity, a commitment to learning and the courage to do it. It would of course be disingenuous of me to suggest I do not see the value of formal training, having devoted over two decades to training actors within a conservatoire-style environment. It has been my passion and my privilege and continues to be so. Every day I am lucky enough to work with some of the best teachers in the sector, training at a world-class level with talented student actors. If it is possible for you to access such training, I recommend it wholeheartedly, but it is *not* essential.

Learning is a joyous and challenging lifetime activity, and you are independently in control of it. Independent means capable of thinking or acting for oneself, not easily lured by the status quo, being a freethinker. Independence for the actor includes being free of subservience to or dependency on a 'master' or 'guru' – becoming an artist in your own right and taking responsibility for your work – such a liberating act. It is not the job of a director or teacher to make decisions for you – it is crucial to develop your confidence and own your independence.

The independent actor is courageous enough to be accountable for their own work and acts as an equal, placing themselves in a space to make choices confidently and without fear. This helps to break traditional hierarchies and helps you own your work as an artist. This may be much easier to suggest than to enact of course, but the systemic issues ingrained in our institutions and our industry will be challenged better if you *fail to comply*. Outdated structures need to be dismantled and you can help by breaking with these traditions. The independent actor leads the way for their peers, ready to collaborate with equity and trust.

Most acting careers include frequent periods of unemployment, of working in other employment and managing a good deal of rejection. Actors learn to be resilient and incredibly flexible in managing their working lives and this is mirrored in our expectations of them when they are engaged in work. On any project, actors come together from differing backgrounds, training routes and work experiences and each engagement creates a unique and new company. This company usually exists for a very limited time and is then dissolved, leaving only production photos, recordings and memories. Despite the social and collective nature of being part of an acting company, the actor must also be self-sufficient, self-motivated and self-determining.

Independence and flexibility are key skills and in screen and recorded media work it is just as vital if not more so than it is in theatre. Invariably, screen work is shot out of sequence so the actor must be prepared to adapt to this. Equally, limited studio time with a cost imperative for radio or voiceover jobs requires the actor to be reflexive in the moment and deliver on time. In either of these scenarios the actor will rarely meet the full company and yet they must tune into the work instantly and adapt as required. The independent and flexible actor will work.

There are many excellent books on acting approaches and techniques and this book does not attempt to explain these in equal detail or indeed to espouse a single methodology. I will reference many of these books as resources in the final chapter. It does not pretend to offer a new system, neither can it incorporate every idea on acting. I believe in a magpie approach to actor development, one which expands your vision rather than restricting you to a single methodology. An open and varied development will serve you as you move between acting contracts and exercise your skills in a wide variety of jobs across the creative industries. As you encounter different creatives and learn from their methods, you will develop your own interests and continue to accrue learning.

Each chapter is designed to be read as a standalone and yet also connects to the other chapters. As an independent actor you are in the driving seat of your own journey and whilst all these topics are inextricably linked, you may prefer to read them out of sequence. The point of this book is to offer up some access as an acting companion from which you can also be steered to other sources and without the pretension of there being a hierarchy of ideas. There are many exercises and tips along the way to help you actively explore the ideas. It aims to demystify the fundamental components of the actors' development and recognise connections between them. It keeps an open view on how skills may be developed with a chapter offering exercises for the self-led actor who may not be working in a group setting. Each chapter signposts the actor to relevant resources enabling them to source specific learning for their development in a transparent, practical and detailed way.

My own route as a practitioner did not start in a conservatoire setting, but rather at an Arts College within a University. Despite this I did work for a time as an actor and did not encounter a conservatoire-style experience until later in my thirties once I was working as a Theatre Director. I took time out to complete my MA at a conservatoire and then returned to my theatre work. Whilst this experience featured as an opportunity to explore my practice and develop, my drive as a practitioner was not the result of time spent there – my drive was born of my own innate curiosity and the need to understand *how* and *what* to practise. I believe the artist will emerge and grow from whatever surroundings they are afforded if their passion to pursue their art is unstoppable.

Whether you choose a formal training route or not, this book advocates for the actor to own a self-led practice, which will nurture you before, during and in between working contracts. There is no shortcut to developing knowledge, understanding and embodying experience. Explanation cannot replace experience. Reading this book can help give you some direction, knowledge and understanding, yet only *you* can improve your practice. Commit to learning by *doing* and growing as an independent actor who is generous, flexible, autonomous and resilient.

The actor is continuously searching for the light bulb moment which illuminates a particular choice or direction. In this book I have tried to encompass my own learning from the discoveries, struggles and fears expressed by the many hundreds of actors I have had the privilege of helping and to analyse the route we found together to illuminate their momentary darkness.

FOREWORD

Treat this book more like the album of a band you never knew you needed, rather than approaching it as a traditional textbook for actors.

Seriously, try it.

Go to the table of contents now and imagine you're browsing a playlist (because you essentially are). Pick a track that catches your eye and just hit play.

I trained as an actor at Mountview nearly two decades ago under Sally Ann's guidance while she was the Head of Acting. Sally Ann is an anti-guru; she'd probably cringe if I sang her praises too much. But 'guidance' in this sense is far from hierarchical. It's about true collaboration. True guidance teaches you to become your own mentor and to develop a process on which you can rely. Reading *The Independent Actor* feels like listening to the greatest hits of possibly the most influential 'band'. To extend the metaphor, I've had these 'songs' on repeat for many years, and they've been the backdrop to my career.

While Sally Ann asked me to write this foreword, I think this speaks more about her values and kindness than it does about me. To illustrate this point, it's essential to share a bit about myself, to give you context and to hopefully make you take my words about this book seriously. I would be classed as a Millennial. I'm from the North East of England where I grew up in a working-class household in a former mining town. I am an actor, writer, director, sound designer, composer, producer and now an agent. I am the founder of Divergent Talent Group. I am also a co-founder of the Obie award-winning theatre company, Dead Centre, with whom I toured the world and was an associate artist for many years. My experiences stretch from the stages of London's West End and New York to major TV series. I've scored films and was one half of transatlantic pop duo BOII.

While preparing to write this foreword, I clambered up into my very dusty attic to discover some old reports from my time as a student. I found one from Sally Ann where she simply wrote, '*A strong process is the most valuable part of the actor's life. You have left no stone unturned in your quest to assemble and understand your process. Never lose your drive, Adam.*' It moved me to re-read this. I remembered that after a lengthy stint as an actor in a West End production, I felt like I'd lost that drive Sally Ann mentioned in the report. In 2012, I called Sally Ann to see if I could come back to teach for a bit, and she welcomed the idea with her typical generosity. Without question, proximity to learning reinvigorated and realigned my drive to create, and this book will do just that for you too.

For me, the guidance in this book has meant finding deep joy in defying easy categorisation; any shame I may have felt previously about doing lots of different things evaporated long ago. Reading this book is a powerful reminder that the life of an actor is never a straight line, but that working on acting *is working on yourself*, both as an artist and as a human.

The Independent Actor is a book for you, for today and for years to come. While this is undoubtedly a quietly political volume, the volume on creativity is loud. Its subtitle '*An Accessible Companion for All Actors*' is no empty slogan either. You will find this book incredibly simple, and yet the pages are dense with meaning. Carry it with you, whatever stage of your career. Take it out of your backpack in a moment of fear, and I know you'll find courage. Pick it up when you're blocked, and you'll have a light bulb moment. If you are looking to shake up or even design and build your actor's process from the ground up, this is without question the text for you. For all the moments in the life of an actor, there is something for you here.

Starlings, like actors, can perform a beautiful murmuration as one giant body, but it can be a trick of the eye. Upon closer examination, both the starling and indeed the actor can only move as one when every individual is in tune with their own independence and when they are in place. To be 'in place' as an actor is not about doing what you are told. It is not compliance or servitude. It is to be in place with your own aliveness of mind, body and spirit. It is freedom. While carving a singular path as an independent actor is necessary, you will only become more meaningfully connected to the world through this process, drawing inspiration from it and changing it.

Adam Welsh, 2024

ACKNOWLEDGEMENTS

Thank you to every practitioner who has believed in my contribution over time. My deep gratitude to Gabrielle Reidy, Lolly Susi and Jennie Buckman – you will continue to resonate in my work. The extraordinary team at Mountview (recent past and present) for whom I hold deep gratitude. To the many hundreds of students I have had the privilege to work with – you are the future of our creative industries. I am humbled by your brightness and feel such joy in tracing your journeys. To those who have become close friends and colleagues – your creativity and kindness keeps me forever on my toes.

To my late dad who gave me my patience and heart, I know how proud you would be. To my brilliant artist mother, Kate, you have been here all the way, encouraging me onwards. To Andrew, my big brother, genius cyclist and rock, to Emily for her care and to awesome Jessie who fills me with hope for the future. Caroline my soul – you knew I would do it and Shira my wise yogi – you knew it had to happen, and Krissy – one love sister. To all the young bright sparks – Phoebe, Emelia, Sophia, Ardi, Marlen, Mabli, Serene, Aine, Ruauri – shine on.

CHAPTER ONE

Training

Whilst an intensive three-year training has long been considered the quality mark for actors – and is perhaps the most straightforward way of accruing your skills – it is not necessarily the right choice for every actor. The world has changed dramatically since the inception of conservatoire-style training and with each generation come new ways of seeing and of reimagining structures. It is a big decision – pursuing your goal in the short term towards a career with infinite possibilities and yet unpredictable prospects.

The route is not fixed; you may choose to learn in a conservatoire environment, a university setting, or as a working actor on a film set, taking classes whilst auditioning, performing in fringe work or curating your skillset at home in a self-led approach. Training is not something that *happens* to you, it is a process activated by you. Whilst it is hard to have complete control over your career, you can take control of how you develop your skills and how you think as an artist.

Only you can set your goals and only you have the power to achieve them, the best coach in the world cannot achieve them for you. Your development as an actor requires both creative and technical input. It is vital to expose yourself to new ideas, approaches, technical knowledge and honest feedback on your work. It is equally important to rely on your own creative resources and imagination. The external resources you draw on, be it tutors, observation, reading, recording, playback or writing will support you in achieving your goals but only *you* can realise the outcome.

The training process is a form of apprenticeship; we learn from experiencing the skills we wish to develop, often in the company of experienced artists and coaches. This ideology frees up the responsibility for learning, giving it to the actor. This does not diminish the role of the teacher but allows them to act as a facilitator rather than a guru. The 'master' or 'guru' infantilises the student actor, making them subservient to their 'power' – whether this is deliberate or not, it is so by design. Such outdated learning relationships are based on mystery and power dynamics and are not only potentially harmful, but ineffective because the learner is not at the centre of the learning.

The word *training* is problematic too. Artistic development requires the actor to feel free to immerse in a flow of creativity and to experiment within their learning. *Training* as an activity is associated with discipline and obedience at its centre; this conjures up notions of military-like regimentation, restriction and hierarchical power dynamics resulting in enforced subservience. These are not useful in our bid to encourage a freethinking creative state, which is dynamic and imaginatively powered. In my experience, learning actors never benefit from hierarchical structures, nor from the regimen that accompanies them. They can learn to imitate and to complete exercises successfully in a power-led training model, but they will lack ownership of their process and ultimately lose interest in it. Commitment, perseverance, reliability, repetition and preparedness are all essential to your development, yet these are learnt through your attention to the creative work – they do not need to be imposed. Curiosity and a passion for the work you are making will naturally create the discipline you require.

The association of *training* with sport is perhaps a more positive one. The role of the coach applies very well to some aspects of actor development and acting coaches can learn from sports science in terms of development and positive motivational approaches. Repetition as a training tool in sport also applies to the technical elements of actor development but it does require a degree of balance. Whilst there are many technical elements that benefit from rigorous repetition to create a muscle memory, it is the exercise of the imagination which is key. Release work, creative freedom and play are your priorities for exercising the imagination, so the facilitation of these is as important as technical coaching. Your development as an actor must be a holistic and creative process of skills assimilation, imaginatively connecting ideas and preparing you for performance opportunities.

Dedicated athletes striving for the highest level of achievement can be seen as a mirror for the aspiring actor but the competitive element in sport is very much out of kilter with the actor's process. The industry is competitive, but the actual work is collaborative, and collaboration is at the heart of the most potent and successful production work across the world. Put at the heart of the actor-training model, it revolutionises the system. Shifting language from *train* to *develop* promotes an ideology for actors to flourish with independence and at their own pace, encouraged by coaches and collaborators. This creates an equal space, offering artistic and knowledge exchange dedicated to those in the room, with shared goals, yet independent responsibility. Language has been a tool of oppression for centuries, if we are to systemically change our relationship to hierarchies and dismantle these structures in the arts, we must own the language we choose. When the learner drives their own development, teachers or coaches feel the freedom to create a more flexible partnership based on the learners' needs rather than adhering to a rigid teaching agenda.

When we treat human beings with equity and without the circus of status play, they thrive. So too for the actor in training. Acting students benefit from the sharing of knowledge and skills made possible by the coach; in turn, they bring an openness, an enthusiasm to learn and a different lived experience. The coach benefits by seeing the work through a new lens and so can develop their practice further. It is a partnership, one from which both coach and actor grow, without the need for power or hierarchy to control it. If you are choosing a self-led approach, the politics of how you are treated can be easier to navigate in some respects, but you will need to choose your collaborators well.

When you are considering your development, ask yourself the following questions:

- Where do you see your future career – what are your ambitions?

- What length of time do you want to commit to realise this development?

- What time, resources and finance do you have available?

Be as realistic as possible in answering these questions. Try to avoid limiting yourself by looking to the example of others – break your own new ground, be independent, these questions are about *your* journey. Do not be influenced by the expectations of others for you or limit your own perception of what is possible. Dream, own that dream and identify how you can best achieve it. Once you have decided the scope of your dream you can plan for how you are going to achieve this within the time frame you wish to give it.

If you are a good decision maker, a great planner, confident and kind to yourself, you may be ideally suited to a self-led approach. If you enjoy relinquishing responsibility for decision making and you do not yet have the confidence to be your own motivator, then drama school could suit you better in your journey towards becoming independent.

The financial aspect of going to a formal training can be daunting; however, even in a self-led approach you will need to be prepared to spend some money. Prepare a plan – assess your current financial position and the cost of the route you are considering. Once the impact is clear, you will know how much income you will need to generate and then you can make decisions. If you are choosing drama school, relying purely on student loans is a risky strategy and I recommend generating some additional income before the course commences. Once the course starts, it will be much harder to find the time to focus on earning money, particularly in your final year as you prepare to launch your career.

Whichever route you choose, you are deciding to become a student and embarking on a wholly transformative experience to become an independent actor. It is useful to weigh up the different benefits gained by either approach. Not all drama school experiences are the same, but this table offers a general picture of what to expect and compares it to a self-led approach:

Choosing Drama School	Choosing a Self-Led Approach
curriculum is already established and tested	you decide what to prioritise
subject specialists and practitioners under one roof	you choose your teachers and empower your own learning

Choosing Drama School	Choosing a Self-Led Approach
practice facilities are purpose built or adapted for use	flexible learning – you choose where, when and how you learn
focussed environment in which to dedicate your practice	you strengthen your independence by creating your learning environment
community of practice – students, staff	you choose your own company
wellbeing support mechanism in place	investment in your own wellbeing is essential
possible funding routes to pay for your development, e.g., bursaries	cost of training is more flexible and less prohibitive
opportunities to perform throughout the course are enshrined	you identify the opportunities, and you negotiate or audition to be involved
exposure to agents, casting directors and other industry professionals	you need to cultivate your own networks and showcase yourself
after care for alumni differs but the School and its reputation remains an anchor	you will need to be more emotionally self-sufficient
innovation of learning, teaching and subject methods are continually revised	you will need to be proactive in discovering and exploring new approaches

Even if you are already at a drama school, the key to your development lies in your decision to become independent and take responsibility for your process. Your tutors can help you much quicker once you take on this responsibility. Ensure you are committing to a growth mindset, free exploration and experiment and it will really help your process. Never be reliant on your tutors for praise – self-sufficiency is a wonderful resilience tool. Recognise your development and congratulate yourself on your hard work.

For some actors, drama school is not an option: financial pressures, time limitations, geographic location or maybe a personal choice to break with the bonds of institutional learning will deter them. The decision to take control over your learning by designing a self-led programme is brave and exciting and will suit some students brilliantly. Beware – choosing to do it yourself is not an easier option and is not for the faint hearted!

Drama school

There is excellent acting training available in many drama schools and colleges and a conservatoire-style delivery can enable you to immerse yourself completely. If you decide on this as your learning route, you will want to identify an established and experienced course with a good reputation that suits your needs. Firstly, do some thorough research to identify your own ranked list of where you may wish to go – explore every option and not just those already familiar to you. Ideally, speak to recent graduates so you have an up to date picture of the training on offer. A close look at website information should outline the shape of each course for you. Try to identify what questions this information *does not answer* and draw up a list of positives and negatives from each, so you can think deeply about your choices and make comparisons.

- What is the primary focus of the course?
- What is the balance of theatre vs screen training?
- Where is the college campus?
- How many places on the course are available each year?
- Who are their alumni?
- What performance opportunities are available?
- What industry support can students expect?
- What welfare and learning support is available to students?
- If you have specific disability needs, what support can you access?
- What accommodation options are there?

If you cannot find the answers, try emailing the admissions team or make a list of questions to ask at your audition. Apply as soon as you are ready and only apply to those that really appeal to you directly. Be open and listen to advice from friends and family but then make the choice for yourself. Apply in plenty of time and start preparing before you apply so you have control. Places are always limited on these courses and setting your heart on one option is quite a gamble. However, settling for a course that is not what you want can also backfire. Remember you can choose to reapply the following year if you do not get an offer that feels right. The offer of a place can feel both exciting and overwhelming, so acknowledge your instinct but discuss it with family and friends before making an impulsive decision.

Getting into drama school can become an all-consuming ambition. We witness new students each year as much relieved by having accomplished this initial goal, as they are excited and nervous to be in a new environment. Equally, the nerves of starting this new challenge can get in the way of you giving your full potential to what has become such a life goal. Remember – a decision to go to drama school is just a steppingstone commitment towards your actual goal! Drama school is not the destination itself. Place your efforts on engaging with as much high-quality experience, understanding and skills development as possible rather than worrying about how hard it has been to arrive at this point or what will happen at the other end of the journey. 'End gaining' is where our mind and actions are ahead of us, where we are striving for the endpoint rather than the moment we are in. This is never helpful for the actor and so proves useful as a first lesson in good acting – be in the present moment (see Connection). This moment is all we have. Lower the stakes, stay focussed on your development and move forward.

Your previous experience at school, tertiary or higher education, youth theatre, and your life experiences generally, all form part of your starting point. If you have already engaged in drama classes, you will have experienced some approaches to acting and perhaps some experience of performing. Whatever is the case, it is essential that you embrace what you do know and be honest with yourself about what you *do not yet know*. We all start somewhere, and it can be liberating to identify what you do not know – it gives you an immediate goal. Many acting students arrive at drama school imagining they are there to polish up their existing skills, and then they experience a drop in confidence when confronted with the challenge of gaining new skills.

Without doubt you will also discover more about yourself during this journey, try to start from a celebration of what you do know of your identity and your passions. Commit to bringing your authentic self to drama school, it is exciting to work with actors who are prepared to bring their whole selves to their training. Training is experiential and will only have the impact you desire if you commit 100 per cent. Bring your curiosity, commitment and courage to the experience and you will achieve your goal of developing as an independent actor and creative artist.

Each year unhelpful myths surface around the notion that drama schools work by 'breaking you down'. If this was ever a reality, it is certainly no longer the case. Each year also brings a newly adjusted rumour about what 'freshers' will be asked to do in their first weeks. Whilst there may be some dubious historical precedent to some of these rumours, in my experience of current training practice, they thankfully no longer represent a reality – it is pure mischief making often on the part of previous students: *'they get you to take all your clothes off and pretend to have a bath in front of the class'* or ' *they lock you in a cupboard to test your vulnerability'*. There is no arguable basis in twenty-first-century training for such an approach and my best advice if you *were* to encounter such nonsense, is to swiftly go in the opposite direction, report it and demand a refund!

Starting at drama school can be anxiety inducing because it is unknown, a new chapter in your journey. It is entirely normal to be anxious when you are approaching a new course in a new environment, and such anxiety can extend to every subject, exercise or assignment required of you. The 'newness' provokes this anxiety by tapping into our deepest fears of failure. A fear (see Wellbeing) that we simply will not understand what is being asked of us – *'perhaps everyone else will "get it" and I will look like an idiot'*. This is *learning anxiety*, which is a normal part of the learning process – embrace it as a catalyst for you to take courage. So, rather than your inner child hanging on for dear life, know that if you take courage to overcome this you will reach a point at which those fears are allayed. They will only return when you encounter more newness!

Most students embarking upon training have experienced a life of compulsory education, after school classes or clubs and may have explored further education on a college course. Drama school is different. Designed as an opportunity to develop a professional practice, it serves as a curated opportunity for exploration and repetition towards a specific vocational goal. It is doing, it is practical. During your training, you will hear truthful maxims which explain this such as 'acting is *action*' or 'acting is *reacting*'. In training, you will gain knowledge and understanding, but simultaneously you will be practising the application of what you learn. In a well-developed curriculum, there will also be an aim to embed an approach that creates new habits to draw upon – this gives you a foundation from which to develop.

Drama school is a constructed environment with a single vocational purpose. When you have settled into the environment and understood the culture there, you will have a clear sense of whether it is the opportunity you had imagined. Check your course handbook thoroughly to understand the whole course trajectory – careful sequencing of learning means there will be some elements you will be introduced to later than others. Elements you see as *missing* may happen at a different point in the training for a sound pedagogical reason. If it becomes clear that a particular element does not form part of the training you are committed to, you can utilise a self-led approach to include it in your journey. This is a positive way to solve the issue – it will prevent you resenting the rest of the course and it will still enable you to achieve your goals.

Practitioners you encounter will have a wealth of learnt ideas, approaches and influences from which they may have created their own innovations. For you to gain the most, you must be open to every approach you encounter, engaging with this work and making sense of it. Our practice comes from our specific experiences, tastes and developed expertise. Whilst it is sometimes possible to trace the provenance of ideas back to a single practitioner or a group of practitioners, the nature of acting practice for the most part survives though an oral or somatic tradition. That is to say that even where there are detailed accounts of practice in acting books, they cannot hold the nuance of *doing*. The act of teaching is a generous one and the content offered to you is yours to use in a way that works for you. The training has only worked if you have a genuine sense of ownership of this work and are able to apply it in practice.

A self-led approach

A self-led approach is exactly what it says – you are leading. Choosing to drive your own learning forwards without the drama school route requires you to rely on your willpower, vision and a personal commitment to being honest with yourself. The self-led approach may be a lonelier process and at times lack the external motivators to keep you going. However, unlike ever before in the history of the world, the information you need to curate your learning is now accessible and there is an opportunity to gain it in a fully flexible way, designed and convened by you. Allowing yourself to be the person setting the goals and working towards them is an exciting prospect. In many respects, if you go it alone, you will have more need of people – a self-led approach should not be a solitary venture! It will also test your leadership skills and this is fundamental on the journey to becoming an independent actor. Grow your possibilities and aspire to be inspirational to others in shifting the paradigm of what acting training looks like.

Consider: You will be responsible for making all the decisions and for monitoring your own progress.

- How will you resolve frustration when certain elements of your practice elude you?
- How honest can you be with yourself about your progress or the gaps in your practice?

Remember that not all learning is the result of teaching led by teachers. Indeed, most learning – and in my experience some of the best examples of deep learning – happen because of practise rather than directly from teaching. Learning happens by watching others, by reading, thinking and reflecting, by practical application of knowledge, by *doing*. Think outside of the box when considering who you will learn from. A self-led approach does not mean you do it all on your own, nor does it mean you should be closed from external input or isolated from others. You will benefit from including the help of professional tutors and you will need to curate your own access to them; the tutor is helpful as a facilitator, to initiate what and how to practise. Surround yourself with people whose generosity will help you grow.

Consider: How will you draw on each of the following resources and identify them as a regular practice?

Yourself – your own resources are without limit, you will have a good deal to offer that is yet unknown to you. You are at the centre of this process and you will be engaging your own resources in every sphere of your work. You are working towards securely establishing your sense of yourself as the source of your acting – establishing your understanding of what performance skills you need to acquire and engaging in regular reflection on achieving those targets. Carefully nurture your technical and creative progress simultaneously to develop. Begin by creating an awareness of your own physical resources as the instrument of communication. By focussing on developing your physical resources first, you will allow your mind to connect to your whole body (see Movement). Develop your background knowledge of drama for theatre, screen and recorded media and be prepared to critically assess your own work and the work of others.

Technology – prioritise the purchase of a computer device so you can utilise popular communication platforms. Ensure the audio and the web camera work and that you have good internet access. Buy an ethernet cable so you can plug in to your router and not simply rely on Wi-Fi. Increasingly, tablets are being utilised in rehearsal rooms so if you can invest in one it will prove useful. In terms of a recording device for audio or visual, a current smartphone can very easily deliver what you need. You may also wish to invest in a camera and tripod set up for recording your work.

Acting buddy – finding an actor friend who understands your journey is helpful. You may already have a friend who would agree to this. If not, then use online networks and forums to identify someone. This is a two-way arrangement that does not involve financial exchange but may lead to friendship and coffee! You can journey together or share your individual discoveries and recommend various stimuli or approaches, offer mutual honest feedback, and be prepared to receive constructive criticism.

Remember that unless someone is brave enough to give you entirely honest feedback, you could be working ineffectively and repeatedly be making the same mistakes. Start by giving your acting buddy explicit permission to be honest with you and offer the same to them in return.

Acting tutor/coach – an acting tutor/coach can be a very useful addition to your resources. This will depend on your financial position and how advanced your practice currently is. Even if you do not employ an acting tutor for an ongoing series of sessions, it is helpful to identify someone who you would trust for a one-off session. An initial assessment with a freelance acting tutor can help you to identify your strengths and your challenges. This could be in person or online so if you are living in a rural area you are not negatively impacted. When looking for a tutor it can help to respond to trusted recommendations from other actors, if you know any. Equally, there are many forums found on interest sites (such as Mandy.com or Backstage.com) where you can ask the opinion of actors who may know someone in your area. Social media can be a very useful way of tapping into a 'hive mind' and getting recommendations quickly. It is also helpful to identify practitioners who work on a freelance basis in a drama school setting. They will have a host of training resources and will have an established understanding of how to help you grow. At an initial assessment, they will also have a useful benchmark to identify the level you are currently working at.

Acting books – you do not need to reinvent the wheel. Whilst acting may feel like an unsolved mystery to you, there are many who have trodden this path of investigation and there is a wealth of written content in existence to support your acting journey. Whilst you will not become a better actor by reading a book, you will discover approaches for your practice that can improve your work. This book outlines areas of practice for you and points you to other resources. Find a library that is prepared to order books in for you rather than you investing money in every book of interest. For many actors, the task of reading entire textbooks cover to cover is a daunting one. There are no rules. Allow your curiosity to lead you, gravitate toward the chapter that first draws you in and you can always read previous chapters retrospectively.

Reading is there to help you; at its best, it should inspire you to action. Reading books about acting or theatre or film allows you to organically develop your vocabulary around the subject, which can be confidence building. If reading is challenging for you, for example, you may have dyslexia, you could choose to listen to audiobooks or podcasts. Try to avoid becoming over cerebral or too philosophical in your attempt to understand the content of an acting book. Instead – and as soon as is possible – try the ideas out on your feet.

Plays and scripts – these will form a key element of your working life and as a learning tool the more you can read across genres and styles the better. Do not limit yourself purely to the type of structure, language or narrative you most enjoy – you will need to push yourself to understand the breadth of possibilities. Reading is a brilliant opportunity to practise your sight-reading (see Text) and this is a fundamental skill for the actor. Reading aloud every day will accelerate this skill. If you take on voiceover work further down the line, you will be cold reading all the time under studio pressures. Read both plays and screenplays to become more familiar with the differences between them.

Online content – YouTube style content has great benefits so ignore the snobbery associated with it and search for 'acting coaching'. From there you will find videos of practical acting sessions on various topics with actors reflecting on their process. The joy of this content is that you can watch it on repeat if necessary, you are in control of pausing it – and importantly if you are working – you are in control of the timing you choose to view the content. The downside is that you do not receive feedback from the tutor on the skills you learn. Internet searches can send you down a rabbit hole, so stay focussed! As you view exercises and practise them, you can record yourself so that you can reflect on them. You can also share your recordings with your acting buddy and ask for honest feedback. Not all content is high quality of course so choose trustworthy sources. Familiarise yourself with internet-created content that employs actors and the range of games that utilise voiceover artists.

Group classes – the tradition in the United States of 'taking class' will become more popular in the UK and Europe as actors become more independent. Drop-in classes at acting studios are available in most major cities of the world. Regardless of where you live, a local arts centre, community arts provision or adult learning centre may provide classes. You may wish to utilise classes for elements such as improvisation, devising work or for performance opportunities. Any group class will enable you to learn and develop group skills, including negotiation, collaboration, listening, and making offers. It will also enable you to measure the level of your skills in the company of other actors. If you are in a more remote location, you could join a local social media forum group and network with other actors. This could lead to you setting up regular in-person meetings to read plays, devise work, discuss reading or exchange experiences. You may choose to research live internet-streamed group classes to join – these are becoming increasingly popular.

Observation of other actors – this may take the form of in-person or online observation of your acting buddy. It is essential to observe the practice of others in order that you do not exist in a bubble. A self-led approach can be lonely and experiencing other actors at work will enable you to position your own understanding and skills more easily. Go to the theatre – lots of it and of all genres. Observe work that is stylistically complex, either in its writing, e.g., verse, verbatim, or in its theatrical conventions, e.g., site specific, unusual seating configurations. It is important to see excellent work and equally useful to see its opposite. Netflix and other streaming services may be associated with your leisure time but they are also useful for actor observation. Structure an element of your week to view television and film as a learning opportunity. Choose an actor to follow, this does not need to be the protagonist, it can be more helpful to observe those in smaller satellite roles. It can also help to avoid well-known actors or those of whom you may be a fan! Use the pause function to help you stop and reflect on a performance and to rewind and examine sequences. Observation is a very useful learning tool, yet remember to develop your own choices authentically – your practice is informed by your own lived experiences; you are not looking to imitate or copy a 'master'.

Observation of real life – 'people watching' is one of the most important activities you can engage in. If you spend too much time around other actors, there is a danger that you can begin to imagine that all people behave as you do. Remember that artists are often more free, liberal and tactile than most because we cultivate and nurture those qualities and values deliberately to benefit our creative practice. Office workers in accounting or insurance or those in retail may not automatically behave in such open and collaborative ways, simply because their environment does not encourage it. By watching as many varied people as possible across the spectrum of age, employment, faith, income background and personality, you will be able to build up a library of behaviours to draw upon in future roles. Observation will help you to make very specific choices contributing to the authenticity of the roles you play.

Observation of other art forms – go to see stand-up comedy, spoken word, music concerts, art galleries, exhibitions, installations, circus and dance – the list really is endless (see Creativity). It will serve several purposes: to brighten your spirit and inspire you, to help you consider form, subject matter, and themes to make connections in the world, to help you connect more deeply as an artist. Through finding connection and inspiration to art forms other than acting you enable your creative spirit to be more expansive and your work to become less derivative.

Journal – use a journal and make notes that will make sense to you without the buddy, tutor, book or other resource. Use it to make notes on your process, learning points and to ask yet unanswered questions. Use it to reflect on why a performance was exceptional or otherwise. Given the opportunity, how would you have approached the role? What is the actor playing the role *doing*? What choices have they made in terms of character, relationships to others and to space? How authentic is the actor? Do they make the narrative believable? How would you approach the emotional journey of this character out of sequence? Refer to your journal throughout your journey.

To design your learning schedule much depends on your prior attainment and what skills need the most development:

- What skills do you currently have and what level are they at?
- What subjects are entirely new to you?

- Considering your current skillset and level, where do you need to place your focus?

- Set desired outcomes for your learning and regularly measure your progress – if you are not sure what you are intending to achieve you cannot celebrate when you achieve it!

You need to decide:

Questions	Consider	Advice
What to learn?	Which subjects and topics do you need to focus on?	Reflect on your previous experience and make a list. Be realistic and ensure you take yourself out of your comfort zone
How to learn?	Do you need a tutor for certain areas?	Use the list to inform which tutors you need and research cost
	What sort of learner are you?	Know yourself and avoid approaching learning in ways that have previously not worked
	Do you respond best to kinaesthetic, aural, reading/writing, visual stimulus?	Factor this in to the way you learn lines for example
	Are you neurodivergent?	What practical adjustments do you need to make?
	Do you have a learning difficulty?	Seek help on advice tailored to your needs
When to learn?	What time do you have available?	Draw up a timetable
	Can you commit to a regular pattern?	The shape of the timetable must reflect your life pattern or you will not stick to it
Where to learn?	Can you use your own accommodation?	Ask family and friends for space if you need it or use a local park space
	Do you have a good broadband connection?	Your local library is useful if you are researching or writing. You can tether a smartphone to help you stay connected on a Zoom call
	Can you access classes locally?	Research local classes at your theatre/arts centre, leisure centre or other community venues

Using headings in this book, schedule your learning as a structured sequence of opportunities to develop your natural abilities. Use your availability as the central pivot around which you build in time to learn and practise individual skills or become involved in a production. Choosing which skills you will develop and organising them into your week with a plan for delivery will enable you to make connections between them as soon as you start learning. Choose the area of skills you develop, organise them by making connections between them and then look after them, keeping them current and ready to use. Try connecting skills rather than considering them each as an end goal.

Usually, we are aware of gaps in our knowledge or understanding; we somehow perceive what we *do not* know. You may also have embedded knowledge you are unaware of, or your understanding at this point may be purely theoretical. Being aware of your starting point is crucial; it will enable you to structure your learning so it includes the right balance of newness. Action is everything for the actor – knowledge and understanding is nothing without the experience of practical application. It can also be helpful to experience new elements of your work in practice first without knowledge or understanding. It can prevent 'end gaining' – trying to guess the result. Discovering by *doing* is fun and is less pressure than trying to put theory into practice. However, to enable your intelligence and integrity to embed in your work, it is valuable to reflect on knowledge and understanding during the process, to deepen your learning and reveal meaning.

When choosing your tutor or coach, take the time to assess their style of teaching. Try to opt for the practitioner who listens more than they speak, who observes more than they demonstrate and who fully understands your goals. They act as a conduit to presenting different topics within a subject, to identifying the learning points required and to creating a series of opportunities for you. They can also act as a motivator, giving you objective feedback, a prompt for further development and answering your questions. The relationship is at its best when collaborative – a non-hierarchical partnership of equals who each brings a different need, skills and experiences to the union. This takes courage on the part of the coach who harbours the power of knowledge and may fear that equal status somehow reduces their position. The actor also requires the courage to take responsibility for their part in the learning contract and to be open.

Allocate yourself a budget for technology, group classes, theatre trips, wellbeing needs and eventually for promoting yourself in a showcase. A self-led approach could benefit from spending a little money on books and clothing but equally you can use a library and make do with the clothing you already own. Costs need not be a barrier and you can delay elements until you can afford them – there is no hurry. Paying for one to one tuition can be expensive and, if money is tight, you can be strategic and choose to have occasional check-ins to monitor your progress rather than regular tuition. It may also be more realistic to save the spending on an acting coach until a point in the journey when you are ready for feedback.

Your priority is space. Your environment will affect your ability to learn. If you cannot afford to hire space, it is worth thinking laterally about the possibilities open to you. Tidying up the garage or loft space if you have one, working in your backyard or local park to ensure you are free to move. You may have friends or family with a larger space than you and who are out during some of the times you are available to practice. Be proactive and ask around – people are kind and will often say yes.

You may have no professional theatre in the village or town you have grown up in, your frame of reference for acting may be purely screen based and drawn primarily from television and streaming platforms. These references are entirely valid and the challenge will be to try and also gain 3D live experience to absorb the spatial and live language of the theatre space. If you are lucky enough to have access, it is important that you see as many live and in person events as possible: comedy, music gigs, orchestral concerts, plays, musicals, live art, political rallies, exhibitions.

Time-management is everything when you are leading your own development. Whether you have the freedom of time or you are working a job alongside your development, we all know that time flies. A timetable is essential, as is the self-discipline to stick to it. How you use your time will directly link to how you measure your progress. Even if your allocation of days and times changes each week, ensure you tick off every accomplished session. It is great for your confidence to see a visual representation of what you have completed.

While practising, focus on the quality of your work rather than the quantity or the duration of your session. Set manageable goals for each day and, if you can, practise during the time of day when you feel most productive. Developing your skills is a lifelong journey; you lose nothing by shaping your schedule around your availability. If it is a priority for you, there is no reason you cannot achieve your goals. Be patient.

Ensure you are creating breaks from your learning, rest is important (see Wellbeing). Breaks enable the learning to filter down and make sense for you, they better enable you to embody the learning rather than holding it cerebrally. You may only have two days a week to focus on your development, but you will still need a week without training to move into a new headspace. The more ordered your routine is the less you need to worry about sticking to it. If time is squeezing you, identify the tasks you need to prioritise, then organise your learning to maximise this time.

Search for as many opportunities to perform as you can. There may be opportunities at your local theatre to be involved in a community production and, whether amateur or professional, the experience is useful. If you cannot find these opportunities where you live, consider connecting with local actors through an online forum to see if you can work on staging material yourselves. Whilst this is a different sort of experience, it will give you many valuable production skills and build your performance confidence. Film it, then once you have some distance from it, make notes in your journal as you watch your performance back.

- What works and why?
- What does not work and why?
- What would you change and how?

It may only be possible for you to take part in online performance opportunities; these too will give you experience, so take any opportunity that presents itself. Listening to audience feedback on your performances is useful to a degree. Remember that your peers, friends and family will be proud of whatever you do and would never wish to hurt your feelings, so may only give you positive feedback. Equally, there may be someone with a less generous agenda whose feedback is not accurate. Listening to people you are not connected to can be helpful, and if you are working with an acting coach, even just occasionally, you can offer them a complimentary ticket to a performance and ask for their feedback. Reflect on the feedback and use it to develop rather than knock your confidence.

Use these performance opportunities to improve your craft and gain experience, rather than to attract industry attention. In the early stages of your development, the profile of the production does not matter; a low-profile production can help you to focus more clearly on your work without the distraction of industry attendees. Once you are ready to attract representation or seek work, then you can place focus on a higher profile production and target your invitations accordingly.

By leading your learning independently, you will spend some of your time wearing the teaching mantle, so challenge orthodox thinking, interrogate plays whose lived experience is different to your own, allow your mind to be changed and for yourself to grow. The value of being open to learning cannot be underestimated; add this to the 3 Cs: curiosity, commitment, courage, and you become powerfully independent.

Learning

Our educational structures put pressure on young people to decide on a singular career path as early as their teenage years if not before. The notion of narrowing our aspirations even before we have experienced the workplace has always seemed a strange concept to me. Creativity is not linear and, in the same way that an acting career can offer you a wide range of acting jobs within the creative industries, the creative industries can also open opportunities to explore your creativity beyond acting. Do not be afraid of these chances, they can develop passions and skills you were unaware of and at the same time offer you new perspectives when you return to acting (see Creativity).

Some people learn new skills quickly, some struggle with application of the learning and yet learn more deeply than others. You are unique. You will have a sense of your own learning tempo, style and needs from years in the education system. Understanding what does not work for you is as powerful as understanding what does. Whether it is performance experience or new skills, avoid making assumptions about the learning as you approach it – assumptions are usually wrong. More usefully, get into the habit of embracing newness and questioning *why* once you have already become involved in the work so you can dig deeper into it.

The decision to train as an actor is usually born from the joy experienced in drama classes at school, the collective enjoyment found in being part of a youth theatre or perhaps a fascination with actors on film. Rarely is acting a pragmatic employment decision or one encouraged by parents or teachers. Indeed, the emotional and financial instability that can come with life as an actor seem good reasons to be deterred. During the Coronavirus pandemic and the threat to the livelihoods of all those engaged in the arts, there was never a more compelling reason to refrain from actor training. Yet even in this unexpected landscape the desire to act has remained, and so too does the intention of many people to work professionally as actors. Perhaps it is because the job of acting is an intrinsically hopeful one – to do it you must be fascinated by people and believe in them, which itself is life affirming.

Most actors in training at drama school are in the 18–25 age group and the system targets this demographic often unconsciously. The pattern of thinking that actors should train at a young age and within a fixed time frame is outmoded. Learning tempos differ regardless of age, experience is unique to the individual and acting is a lifelong learning pursuit. The value of training at a later age cannot be underestimated – there is enormous value to you and to the industry in approaching it once you have had more life experience. There is also the option of postgraduate training as an older student, which can be a rich experience full of artistic revelation and intellectual connection. But if you feel the desire to devote three years to focussed development, do not shy away from applying for three-year courses.

I have had many experiences of working with actors choosing drama school as a training route in their forties and beyond. Without exception, the life experiences they bring enable them to consider their personal development on a deeper level. They can also usually shed greater light on the actions of characters they are playing. Their innate understanding of empathy and their ability to engage it comes directly from life experience, often paired with a quiet understanding that humans are not invincible, and that life is unexpected.

Whichever way you approach your development, give up on the hurry, take your time and relax around the necessity to nail every skill in a time-limited vacuum. Learning is not a linear activity, it is better represented by a spiral. You begin at the base in the centre of the spiral, accrue knowledge at different stages, which sometimes you revisit – there is no end point of success but rather a wealth of accrued rounded expertise which represents your journey. This is another good reason for the actor to keep a journal. A book with all your learning and reflections in, character studies, stimuli from exhibitions or performances, advice from yourself *to* yourself as an artist as you grow. Use your journal, let it become a go-to companion.

Writing of character ages for screen and stage is increasingly becoming more diverse. From child actors to nonagenarians there will be potential acting roles – do not allow your age to be a barrier to training or to working as an actor. If you do encounter ageism in a casting scenario, just remember it is they who are behind the curve; do not tolerate it and give feedback to your agent to flag it. As an actor beginning your journey at an older age, you may well choose a self-led approach. Remember that your previous life experiences will be vital to you so do not discard them simply because you are starting a new journey.

Past

Every conversation, every action, every relationship, indeed your entire life to date has been a learning experience which is filed in the library of your mind and body. Your life experiences hold directly transferable learning from situations. Part of developing as an actor is to widen your experience of life and people as much as possible and to spend time exploring your own identity, beliefs and values (see Connection). Knowing yourself and starting from a transparent and honest place enables you to learn on a deeper level (see Character and Wellbeing).

There are also socio-political–historical–economic factors beyond your control which have an impact on how you think and how you see the world. Once we recognise what our worldview is and where we may harbour bias, we can begin to explore what is beyond these held beliefs. Your work as an actor will mean you collide with innumerable scenarios, which may be in or outside of your experience. For example, the global pandemic made us all face an entirely new way of conceiving the world. The experiences you captured during this time will be a valuable resource because they have helped to shape your view on the world.

Present

In the present we hold a wealth of prior learning. Remember you are never starting from scratch. From this position you can question what new learning you want to engage in. How familiar are you with current culture, art, theatre, film, television, streaming platforms, podcasts, current affairs, exhibitions, installations, social justice campaigns? What is in the zeitgeist? What is being talked about on the global stage? What new books have been published? What new plays have been produced? What scientific breakthroughs are there?

Even once you are working as an actor, every day is a learning opportunity (see Creativity). When did you last take a class on improvisation, mask work, script analysis? Have you explored puppetry, voiceover animation, motion capture? Are you reading new scripts? What artistic work is your community engaged in and can you get involved? Community involvement can offer you the opportunity to share your skills. It is accepted that we learn the most when we teach others; find opportunities to pass on your skills – just articulating them helps your own understanding.

Being present is a lesson that not only applies to acting (see Connection), it must also apply to your life. Being present enables you to fully embrace opportunities and move forward into the future – which after all will also become your present. You have an entire lifetime to develop your acting skills if you choose to. Setting artistic goals is useful; work towards them and record your development in your journal so you can reflect on your progress and understand your creative challenges (see Creativity). Build resilience and grit by being out in the world so you can set your goals and pursue them no matter how hard it is. Push yourself beyond your comfort zone and then reflect on your achievements. Be proactive not reactive, dare to dream big and aim high – what is the worst that can happen?

Future

Commit to a future where learning plays a fundamental role. Ring-fence regular time to develop and make it non-negotiable in terms of moving it – protect your creative future. There may be goals that you do not yet feel ready to pursue. Keep a note of these and re-visit them in the future. In every decade try to conquer at least one new skill and stay inspired. There are numerous inspirational speakers you can source online and clips of actors talking about their craft. Read biographical accounts of other actors – this will also help to centre you on your goals. Do not try to predict the future, allow it to surprise you, if you have prepared for it and laid the foundation stones it will lead you somewhere. Embrace where you land and stay open to the next surprise.

Embracing technology

In 2020 when the Coronavirus pandemic struck, the arts sector across the world struggled to survive through the lockdowns, related restrictions and then the reticence of live audiences to return. Theatres closed, rehearsals were cancelled and filming schedules were suspended. Agents had little need to represent new actors and for many their books were paused for signings. It was hard at times to believe this picture would shift and many actors changed their career either temporarily or forever, choosing to study politics, creating a home craft business, or becoming a fitness coach. Yet even in these troubling times, creativity continued to prevail, and the sector is reviving.

Zoom, Teams and media streaming platforms became the overnight key not only to communication but also to industry survival. Artists quickly transformed communication tools into performance platforms and rather than simply discussing creative projects on them, they launched and live-shared their creative projects. Across the world, these experiments explored how creativity could survive and flourish within such new parameters. The results were life affirming. Simultaneously, the already growing trend for self-tape auditions exploded. Suddenly, actors were required to become self-tape experts and singers developed a new command of technology as they sang on camera to backing tracks from their kitchens. Actors finally created the home voiceover studio they had often contemplated, and television and radio productions sustained their output by offering home recorded or hybrid studio shows with a live audience on Zoom.

In this moment, a new era was born for artists across the world. One in which they could become more independent in creating their own work and where accessibility of exposure at last became a reality. For those actors who do not have access to devices or the internet, the technology revolution is incredibly difficult to embrace as it leaves them behind. If you are training in a drama school environment or a university setting, make sure the staff are aware of your technology needs. Is there a learning support fund you could access to help you purchase equipment? This technology prerequisite has become so important, so at the outset of your training journey, prioritise your technology set-up before anything else. If you are crowdfunding, make the technology your priority – it is a learning tool, it can create employment for you and it will be a significant promotional tool for creating opportunities.

Technology often divides us into those who feel confident with it and those who do not. Either we are excited by the fact it is constantly changing, updating and innovating or we find it daunting. Whichever side of the fence you naturally fall on, challenge yourself to embrace technology. It will keep changing and there is nothing to fear; it exists to help you and not hinder – and I say this from a position of not being particularly 'tech savvy' myself! Unless we embrace this progress, we do not benefit from its developments and, perhaps more importantly, become left behind culturally, lacking important understanding of new working processes. New online modes of learning such as podcasts, webinars and live coaching are developing frequently and as soon as they are established, there will be something new to replace them. Embrace it.

On one level, the actor only needs space, passion and a script or other stimuli to work with; such resources help you create, imagine, experiment, repeat and refine your work. Yet consider how valuable a resource the use of recording is to us today. To record your work by audio or film is an immediate feedback tool and currently underused in the training context. We may make use of the facility to record during the final stage of performance preparation and film our performances, but it has far greater use as an immediate feedback opportunity on the specifics of your work.

It can help to hone your measurement of progress – does it *read* for an audience? What is the audience *experience*? Particularly now that acting style is less wedded to naturalism, if you are breaking the fourth wall (see Text and Space) to speak directly to your audience, use recording to help you master this. By reflecting on *actual* recordings of your work, you can become your own critical friend and reject a selective memory of your work. This helps you to gain confidence whilst also giving you the opportunity to improve before others see your work.

I am not referring to the preparation of self-tapes here, those are specific recording opportunities with an external brief and for which you are often naturally playing directly to the camera. The use of self-tapes in the creative industries for casting and for many drama school first round auditions has become standard. Use this to your advantage. You choose the recording, you are not being seen on your first live take, unless you choose this. As ever, preparation is everything. Film yourself making different spatial or physical choices, exploring character traits and vocal use. Playback of these will inform how you choose to develop your performance. Actors can also overthink self-tapes they create and be extremely critical of their appearance and performance on the recordings. This can contribute to low self-esteem and a sense of failure for not having achieved an idea of *perfection*, which of course does not exist. Embrace imperfection, it is far more interesting – allow your self-tapes to reveal your humanity rather than your vanity.

CHAPTER TWO

Wellbeing

Wellbeing practices uniquely link to the skills an actor is developing, such as finding a sense of centre, controlling breath, enabling release, finding flexibility of mind and body and being in the present moment (see Connection, Movement, Voice). Globally we understand the importance of mental and physical wellbeing across a range of workplaces and education set-ups and for the actor it is no less essential. You use your mind and body as a vessel for your art. To achieve authenticity, you open your heart and soul and create emotional connections to imaginary circumstances. You will also draw on the embodied memory of your own lived experiences, both consciously and unconsciously. You will rigorously explore your imagination and invite any number of catalysts to spark it. Most usually, you will do this in the presence of and together with virtual strangers. All of this can be incredibly exposing and so before you engage on this journey of creative exposure, consider how best to look after yourself.

To manage your wellbeing and to thrive in the challenging conditions of your chosen occupation, self-awareness is essential. If you commit to truly knowing yourself, you will be open to listening to the signs your body and your mind give you. The self-aware actor aids their acting process by being alive to *how* they are and *who* they are, and this promotes their own wellbeing in the process (see Connection). As an independent actor you must know yourself, your mind, your body, and act independently to nurture yourself. It is no one else's responsibility but yours. Engaging in self-care is a relatively new concept, mistaken perhaps as selfish action; it has taken a long time to land in mainstream thinking.

Unless prepared for the pressures inherent in the creative industries, these pressures can have negative effects on your ego. The reality of waiting for other people to make decisions about your working life can create self-doubt or, in rare moments of public recognition, you can grow an unrealistic expectation of your future based on media noise or flattery. Becoming an independent actor means becoming resilient and grounded, confidently able to assert your place in the rehearsal room, on set, in the theatre, sound booth and in the industry generally. It means having your own best interests at heart and realistically it will help you to remain in control of managing your ego.

Imagining that acting can offer an escape from yourself is a dangerous approach. At times you may well use this tactic (goodness knows I am sure we all have!) and in certain circumstances it may prove positive in its results; but to rely on it for any length of time can leave you and your identity in a vulnerable and fragile place. The career is tough and the more you can build resilience to it the better. Having a grounded sense of self and being true to your identity are key factors in building resilience. The resilient actor can separate their self-esteem, confidence and expertise from the exposing nature of the business. Resilience through this approach is more likely to ensure longevity. Actors are a generous and caring tribe, and they are interested in other people, so you will never be alone.

Begin by focussing on your physical wellbeing and you will automatically start to help your mental wellbeing; the mind and the body are inseparable. This holistic approach can help motivate you in nurturing your mental health: the more physical activity you engage in, the more oxygen is available to the brain and the more energy you will have in both mind and body. Your body is unique to you – celebrate its possibilities rather than worrying about what it may lack. When your mind and body are working in harmony, you have greater control of their wellbeing.

Fitness – the fit actor will be able to bring a much more energetic offer to their work and to their mental health. Advocates for different fitness regimes will best explain their relative positive impacts and this information is widely available. You may wish to consider adopting an individual exercise or a team exercise or indeed both. By engaging in solo and group activities you can exercise mindfulness whilst flexing your team skills. Avoid overbuilding muscle in a gym-style workout. Whilst it can produce strength, it also produces rigidity – a solid muscle base makes you less agile, nimble and flexible and increases muscle tension. Fitness activity that involves being in the fresh air is invaluable to your holistic wellbeing and aids your concentration.

Fitness will give you flexibility, energy and stamina, all of which will enable you to do your best work. We each have different body shapes and abilities, and casting directors will be looking for exactly that. When you are considering your fitness level do not confuse this with some notion of the need to lose weight or change shape – you already have everything you need, just keep it in good health! Alongside your choice of activity, remember classes in Yoga, Qi Gong, or Tai Chi, all of which will give you fuel for mind and body and complement your acting practice.

Vocal health – the actor is lost without good vocal health (see Voice); it is equal in comparison to the foot health of a dancer – essential for work. Your vocal folds, also commonly known as the vocal cords, are two bands of smooth muscle tissue, found in the larynx, otherwise referred to as the voice box. Air passes from the lungs up through the vocal folds, which vibrate to create sound. If not cared for, these folds can dehydrate and become inflamed and irritated. If your voice sounds hoarse or husky for a prolonged period and you are less able to vary your vocal pitch range, it is usually a sign of poor vocal health.

If you 'lose your voice' it may be the result of laryngitis (laryngeal inflammation), so make an appointment to see your doctor. Alongside other advice such as gargling with salt water, they will usually prescribe a short period of voice rest. If you are hoarse and husky in tone, this is a sign of poor vocal health or an indication of damage, so it will be valuable to have a consultation with an ENT (Ear, Nose and Throat) specialist. They will investigate the cause; they may check for hard or soft growths on the vocal folds – nodules or polyps – and treat them accordingly. In many cases, nodules and polyps are entirely preventable if you commit to good self-care; in some cases, they may require surgery. Never self-diagnose, trust the experts and follow their advice.

As with any condition, prevention is better than cure and as part of your self-care routine include looking after your vocal health.

Hydration is essential, so drink plenty of water and other fluids. This is especially important if you drink caffeine and alcohol, which can have a dehydrating effect on the vocal folds. Smoking, eating before sleep, shouting and screaming all take their toll on vocal health (see Voice).

Self-care – this looks different to everyone and need not be the cliché of long baths and a face mask! Treat yourself with generosity and warmth as you would a loved one. Choose to be in a motivating environment and surround yourself with motivated people; detox by choosing not to spend time with people whose energy you feel is toxic. Challenge yourself to work on a detoxing of your use of smartphones, tablets, laptops and other screens. Try to spend at least one day a week removing yourself entirely from screen use and spend the day in nature. If you live near the sea, go to the beach or a coastal path or, if in a rural environment, go out to the fields or through woods if you can. If you are in an urban space, find local parks, ponds or pedestrian spaces to enjoy the outdoors. The role of nature in enlivening our connection to others and in promoting exercise and mental wellbeing is essential. Try to encounter each of the elements every day in some form – earth, air, water and fire.

To give extra focus to your mental wellbeing, it can help to write a stream of consciousness in your journal each day for all your collected thoughts to have a place. This can free up space in your mind and protect your sleep time. If you are touring or away from home filming or in a regional production, you will need to get used to sleeping in 'digs'. The quality of the room and comfort of the bed will usually depend on how much money you are prepared to spend. It is worth investing more if you are someone who struggles to sleep easily or well. Take a sleeping eye mask, a scented candle, a hot water bottle and ear plugs in your suitcase to help ensure a good night's rest. If you are filming, you will get used to early starts of 4 or 5am, so look at how you can maximise your sleep to ensure your optimum performance. Consider doing small things to best serve 'future you' – make your bed in the morning so it is ready to nurture you at the end of the day, do the washing up before bed so 'future you' does not need to deal with it in the morning.

Cooking fresh food rather than processed foods or takeaways is a good way to remain well and healthy. Try to eat a balance of food groups to give you the energy you need and try to avoid fad diets and trends. Food is essential to life, as ancient as humankind and a precious commodity; whatever your relationship is to food, always remember it is the fuel for all you do. Cooking and eating as activities can bring great joy and are a wonderful way to bring people together with nurture and joy.

Holistic approach

The term Holistic Learning is recognised as a specific learning style, one in which the student intrinsically thinks deeply and widely around the information presented to them. I am using the term holistic here as a *deliberate* approach to learning rather than as a learning *style* particular to the individual. Acting intersects so many parts of your whole being and brings your previous experiences together with your present ones to reveal your identity or inspire your imagined manifestations. So, in your approach to acting, allow yourself to be the starting point and deliberately open yourself to the world from which you can draw inspiration. The word holistic means an interconnectivity of parts, which only make sense in reference to the whole.

Your acting development is not compartmentalised, it does not stand alone from your home life, your relationships, working life or indeed the current socio-political and economic landscape. Your learning therefore can only ever be a part of who you are and how you see and experience the world. Changing your worldview is possible of course but is either a deliberate choice prompted by a catalyst or the result of new impactful experience – nothing happens in isolation. Reflection is an important part of the holistic approach, and it allows you to acknowledge change and create new thinking. It is an art and an essential part of your practice. By taking a consciously holistic approach to your development as an actor, you are accepting all of this and at the same time prioritising your wellbeing.

Many practitioners will ask you to leave your life at the door of the studio and focus solely on the work. To an extent this makes some sense, you need focus, you need to be open to the joy in the room, to experience play, and leave worry, grief and busy schedules at the door. This can give you a wonderful opportunity for respite, but it is not always realistic to relinquish consciousness of the rest of your life for the sake of your art. For a short period, yes, it may be possible to leave your life at the door, but you are the sum of all the parts of your life, and you must be honest with yourself. When we accept this, we can learn authentically and more deeply. To incorporate and embrace your feelings *in* your work rather than reject them and park them at the door can be a courageous choice. The only real caveat here is to avoid these feelings affecting those you are working with – remember they too have a life they are balancing!

Training as an actor has historically been based on devotion and the love of your art being the ultimate sacrifice. Devotion does not make you a better actor – enjoyment, focus and careful attention will do that – devotion is akin to worship, which in my view has no place in any rehearsal room. Some students struggle when they experience the thing that they started doing because it was joyful and fun, becomes a thing they are assessed on, feeling that the thing they love has become a commodity. Of course, the purpose of such assessment is simply to measure progress to offer feedback for improvement. No one will ever ask you for grades in an acting context. It has been common in the sector for acting students to work up to 12-hour days with the underpinning idea that it will give them stamina to enter the industry. Devotion of this kind is not necessary; committing to 12-hour days is good for no one. Quantity does not equate with quality – in life or in art. Indeed, it more usually forces you into unhealthy eating patterns, self-doubt, and endless caffeine to stay awake!

In fact, unless you are fortunate enough to have a career that launches immediately and at high velocity, the stamina you will need is more to do with the resilience of waiting. Waiting for opportunities, waiting on your agent, waiting for the next self-tape, waiting on a recall, waiting on decisions owned by other people, waiting on set, waiting for a film release. Learn to cope with this inevitable pattern of waiting by scheduling your learning time and ensuring you ring-fence time off for yourself. Carefully scheduling your development now will prepare you well for carefully scheduling your working life as an actor. If you are at drama school in training, it is less easy to have ownership of your schedule, but you can organise your time outside of the institution.

A self-led actor needs to consider the best way to organise time. For example, if you have young children or perhaps young siblings in your living environment you may wish to wait until they are in bed before you engage in concentrated practice; whereas if you need to practise a song you may prefer to do this when they are awake. Everything relates to our live circumstances – if you need to take your dog out then practise your lines in the park. If you have research to engage in, go to the library where you will not be disturbed and you may have useful resources around you. This is not about multitasking; it is about synchronising your activities so you can maintain balance. A holistic approach enables you to be organised in a bespoke way and to take control of your continued learning (see Training).

Change

Change for many people is anxiety inducing and if you are not someone who automatically embraces change, it can be scary. The ability to embrace change is powerful, for actors it is a superpower. It is a deliberate choice to become better at thriving on change and once you practise the choice it will become an exciting part of your life. Acting is not a single job – it is a lifetime of contracts of different shapes and sizes. Therefore, your chosen life will be filled with change, not only as you move between contracts but also as you work with constantly changing creative teams and actors. If you approach this with a positive mindset, this can be the very best part of being an actor when you are working; there is never time to become complacent or bored with your setting or those around you.

It may be that rather than not liking change, you long for familiarity. If this is the case, you can easily create the conditions that will enable you to experience familiarity in new settings. Particularly if you are on tour when the newness remains constant, having objects, clothing or habits to spark familiarity is helpful. For example, I used to have a pair of rehearsal socks that would help ground me emotionally in a new space. Whatever works for you is the answer and even a mascot can be a comfort! When you are not working, the lack of change can be infuriating, so finding a place of calm in which you accept these circumstances too will do much for your wellbeing.

Familiarity breeds confidence and confidence is powerful when dealing with change. It enables us to keep trying because we have every reason to believe we can succeed in our goals – confidence is the key to surviving the newness. Confidence can help you to feel in control of change. You can initiate change; it is not just something that happens to you. It may be a change in your working process, a change to how you practise your skills or a change in attitude to performance. You can also be the change – if there are not enough female parts, join a writers' group or start writing your first script (see Text)! Be an actor who actively works to change the landscape rather than one who sits at home and rages. Be confident and know that change is an opportunity.

Fear

Your working life is unpredictable at best with new situations, new people and new challenges regularly, or attending multiple castings yet still waiting for the rare chance of employment. All these factors – even the ones that are equally exciting – are potential causes of anxiety. Anxiety is a reaction of the mind and body to unfamiliar, stressful or risky situations. It produces a feeling of unease or even dread in advance of an event or situation, at its worst it can have a paralysing effect. For you, the developing actor, it is important to recognise the existence of learning anxiety as a very normal experience. Much of what you encounter will be new and will have the power to change you in some way. Anxiety can make you resist the need to learn new skills, yet only by recognising the need to learn these new skills can you take the courage to overcome learning anxiety.

Some level of anxiety is a healthy reaction to life, helping us to remain aware and alert. It acts like an alarm and prioritises our need to consider what is ahead of us. When we have felt anxious and then gone on to achieve well in the scenario we were dreading, we feel a great sense of achievement. However, when anxiety levels are high, the mind and body can struggle in a way that is not good for the health and neither is it sustainable. Fear is the enemy of creativity, bringing with it only a dangerous state for both mental and physical health. When you are learning it is essential to avoid its impact, it has the power to force you to limit yourself and to skew your perception of your goals. Fear has the power to kill creativity in yourself and in others and can encroach on your wellbeing. It emerges from self-doubt, a lack of confidence or when you are approaching new learning – and it can spread very quickly.

It also rears its head when you spend too much time admiring the work of other actors at a similar stage to yourself whilst ignoring your own growth and innate talent. It can create unfounded jealousies that result in negative feelings for yourself; in turn, you project these onto others and ultimately feel guilty for it. This process is exhausting, and you do well to protect yourself from it. It creates a toxic energy that can only have a negative impact on you. It can also leave traces of anxiety that sit in anticipation of fear taking over once again. There is a mythical notion, that to be an actor you must identify as an extrovert; it is not true – many of our greatest actors are introverts and experience feelings of shyness and social anxiety.

Even once the actor is working and established in their career, fear can take hold:

- Why did I not get a recall?
- Why did they cast her rather than me?
- Did they cast me because they ran out of options?
- Will I be able to deliver this role?
- If I fail in this role, will I ever work again?
- If I do work again, will I ever be as good?

You can plague yourself with worry yet still not be able to answer these questions because the answers are not in your control. Solutions for avoiding fear will very much depend on you and your own unique context. There is a plethora of self-help books on the market if that is your thing, or it may be very helpful to seek out a talking therapy to help with strategies and to express your feelings safely – or hypnotism, or meditation or exercise or painting or any other action that will help you specifically to exorcise it. The answer will be as individual as you are – only you can identify how to harness positivity, so it is a force to protect you from fear. Fear is a key human emotion so we cannot erase it as part of our experience, but we can learn to disregard it or use it to fuel a positive outcome.

Adrenalin is a hormone that releases into the body when we feel extreme emotions. Experiencing the effects of adrenalin regularly is part of being an actor and it is essential for you to learn how to best harness this rush of energy for yourself. You will experience this at auditions, in rehearsals, when you are improvising and of course before and during a performance. Do not ignore it, use it and make it work for you. Allow yourself to experience the sensations adrenalin brings to the body and know there are survival options available to you. Research into post-traumatic stress disorder (PTSD) has explored the reactions of animals and humans to adrenalised events resulting in reactions of fight, flight, freeze, fawn or flop.

From a performance perspective, it is interesting to consider this framework so you can understand those instincts in the roles you play. When experiencing adrenalin prior to performance, do you want to confront it, rush away, freeze, appeal to others or give up entirely? The only useful option for the actor is to fight, to confront it head on even when it feels counterintuitive. Imagine this as a choice between excitement and terror – if you choose the positive route, it can open possibilities for the energy you bring into the space. When the 'butterflies' or 'needles' or 'fog' (or however you personally experience it) arrive, remind yourself this is the sensation of *excitement*. Go further, when others ask you how you are feeling, tell them you are *excited* and allow yourself to associate this word with sensation. By mapping the sensation to a positive emotional state, you will be able to ground yourself more easily and take some control.

Establishing a coping mechanism for adrenalin and addressing your fears is a way of demonstrating self-care. The stakes are nearly always lower than we think. If you try a new skill and fail, the impact is relatively small other than the effect it has on your ego, which can perceive it to be a much bigger impact. If you try to approach the new task or skill with a focus on discovery rather than success, it can be far more liberating. You may be inexperienced, but this does not mean you cannot become highly capable at this skill with practice. The desire to learn can fuel you and neutralise the impact of initial failure, turning it into great learning. The act of controlling it positively will also help you to focus more fully on the work at hand. Seeing a project through or persisting through rejection builds your resilience and will improve your sense of self-worth.

Practise being kind to yourself, remember that kindness is contagious. Start with yourself, identify what this can mean, make a list, and treat yourself with words or actions – kindness is the greatest antidote to fear. Free any judgement on yourself or on others and relish the freedom this gives you to build your confidence. Finding opportunities to exercise your sense of humour is also invaluable, we must take our work seriously but never forget our work is to play – so enjoy it, share laughter, exercise wit, offer smiles. Practise making positive comments about yourself; this may be in the form of self-affirmations in private or conversations more broadly in company – if you cannot be confident about yourself, it will not instil confidence in you from others. You can hold the power to transform your approach to your life as an actor and these positive steps will leave you changed.

If acting itself continues to produce extreme anxiety levels for you, it is important to reconsider it as a career. Perhaps you would prefer to keep it as a hobby, or work within the industry in any number of other roles that are not in the spotlight. Your health is far more important than your career and there are other ways to explore your creativity and make an artistic contribution. If you choose to continue to work as an actor, then there are ways in which you can help yourself.

Calm

Each of us finds calm in different ways and there are no rules. A sense of calm is essential to find equilibrium for actors who spend a lot of time raising their adrenalin levels. It is much easier to focus when you have a calm default and this can positively influence your practice. Writing in your journal can really help to establish a sense of self from which you can help yourself achieve a state of calm.

Mindfulness is also helpful to engender a sense of calm; noticing what is happening in the present moment and without judgement. It will also improve your acting by allowing you to be present and to be accepting of difficulty and surprise as you encounter it. Meditation is the oldest form of mindfulness and enables you to create a space for reenergising and clearing the mind. Most meditation is practised in a sitting position and in a waking state of consciousness while focusing the mind and allowing thoughts to come and go.

Moving meditations are also very helpful, allowing continuous movement to aid this focussed state. Guided meditations include self-led meditation using your internal voice or a teacher, in person or on a podcast. Working towards being your own guide is very helpful and allows you to practise independently. Engaging in meditation as a mindfulness activity encourages your thoughts to release. There are various mindfulness apps in the marketplace and if they are appealing to you, try them.

Sleep is the time when we can process our busy lives and regenerate physically; regular meditation practice improves sleep as the mind has more opportunities to process thoughts, feelings and events. Yoga Nidra is an alternative to meditation practice and is a deeply relaxing experience. Usually lying down in a deep state of relaxation with awareness, you move between consciousness to dreaming and back while you remain awake. It is like some meditation practices, but it is usually more structured.

Whichever way you prefer to access it, a degree of peace, stillness and quiet reflection is invaluable in our busy world full of overthinking and overdoing. If you are religious or engage in a spiritual practice, you may already have natural moments of prayer that help you. If not, the list of possibilities for finding peace is endless and everyone has the power to engage with it. A silent retreat is a fantastic way to consider your life deeply and, for the actor, these times of stillness and reflection can be invaluable, deepening your connection to life.

Prepare and rehearse outdoors when you can – script analysis does not need to happen in a closed room. Birdsong and fresh air are inspiring and enliven your mind, allowing you to remember you are alive and spontaneously affected by the world around you. Communion with nature generally is necessary to help you keep perspective and find peace. Whether you can engage with it during your work or in your free time, it will revive you. Get muddy. I used to take my students up to the local park in summer and get them to roll down hills or climb the trees. The thrill of engaging in the live environment was an experience they could then bring to their work with energy, life and wellness. Live in your environment and not in the world of the play until you need to. Environments in which actors spend too much time are black airless studio boxes, theatres defaulting to blackouts during technical rehearsals and sound booths and sets with artificial light. Therefore, when you do not need to be in these environments try to find their opposite.

The wellbeing jar

Write on separate pieces of paper activities that make you feel good mentally, emotionally, physically. They can be detailed or open to interpretation, an instruction, a quote or an open offer. Fold each piece of paper, put it in a large jar and shake it up. Choose a time such as after breakfast to pick a note from the jar and engage in its suggestion.

Examples:

Stretch your body
Embrace the weather
Visit the park
Write a to do list
Tidy your space
Dance
Move in silence
Visit a baby or child
Phone a loved one
Share an inspiring quote
Spend time listening to the healing power of music
Have a paper day (no screens)
Prioritise your to do list
Stroke a pet

Being proactive in developing your wellbeing: fitness and resilience will both aid your acting process and help to promote wellness. Build your self-awareness by answering the questions in the following quiz as a good starting point:

1 Fitness – How fit are you?

    A I could take part in a dance class without running out of breath

    B I could take part in a dance class and would need to pause regularly

    C I could take part in a dance class and would need to watch most of it

    D I could not take part in a dance class

2 Resilience – How resilient are you?

    A I have a strong sense of self and I feel very confident

    B I have a good sense of self and know I am capable

    C I have a sense of self and sometimes feel capable

    D I have little sense of self and often feel incapable

3 Calm – How calm are you?

    A I am always grounded and in complete control of my breathing

    B I am often grounded and I know how to control my breathing

    C I am sometimes grounded and can struggle to control my breathing

    D I am rarely grounded and cannot control my breathing

4 Mindfulness – How mindful are you?

    A I can sit in silence and pay attention to the present moment

    B I can sit in silence briefly and pay attention to the present moment

    C I can sit in some silence and struggle to pay attention to the present moment

    D I cannot sit in silence and rarely manage to pay attention to the present moment

5 Nutrition – How nutritious is your eating?

    A I eat regular nutritiously balanced meals with lots of fresh fruit and vegetables

    B I eat mostly nutritiously balanced meals with some fruit and vegetables

    C I eat nutritiously balanced meals sometimes

    D I eat whatever meals I want to, regardless of nutrition

6   Sleep – How well do you sleep?

    A   I can easily sleep soundly and uninterrupted and I feel rested

    B   I can sleep well without much interruption and feel somewhat rested

    C   I rarely sleep uninterrupted and I wake up feeling tired

    D   I can hardly sleep, I am always interrupted and I feel exhausted

7   Hydration – How hydrated are you?

    A   I drink plenty of water every day and abstain or limit my alcohol/caffeine intake

    B   I drink water every day and rarely drink alcohol/caffeine

    C   I drink water most days and I enjoy drinking alcohol/caffeine

    D   I rarely drink water and I drink alcohol/caffeine more frequently

- If you are scoring A or B for most of these questions, you are clearly taking your wellbeing seriously. You can now enjoy maintaining this and challenging yourself further.

- If you are scoring B or C for most of these questions, you clearly have an awareness of protecting yourself and promoting your wellness. Try to make small adjustments to increase this.

- If you are scoring C or D for most of these questions, you could help yourself by considering your lifestyle choices. See it as an opportunity to form new habits.

- If all your answers are D it is likely that the demanding life of an actor may have negative effects on your health. Seriously consider the value of wellness as one of your goals for your long-term health.

CHAPTER THREE

Creativity

You are an actor and therefore a creative artist. Celebrate this whenever possible – being a creative artist is the part of your work that allows you imaginative freedom, independence, and a voice. Most creative endeavour seeks to offer solutions, to heal, to celebrate, to inspire, to reveal truth, to provide a mirror. The actor's part in this is not small. As the vessel for the words and ideas of writers, filmmakers, directors, or producers, you will also want to bring your own creativity to manifest the work – only the actor can make it live. Sometimes this is in the shape of finding research that informs your creative choices, or it may be through your own human connection and experience of the subject matter. You will be using your intellect, your instinct, your passion, and your integrity to bring stories to life – this is art.

Originality is possible. There are those who tell you there is no such thing as originality – they are wrong. Your unique experience and skills collide with a thought or an idea that is new to you and creates an original fusion. Your perspective and your connections are unique to you. Therefore, your artistic expression is always original. Learning to trust your creative instinct will come with increased confidence. Your gut is always right; the difficulty is that we do not always understand why it is steering us in a particular direction. This is when trust is most essential – when you are not able to rationalise your work. Try to remove your internal voice that wants to control and decipher reason; the reason for a choice is immaterial when instinct is driving it and it always makes sense in the end.

You can also make work yourself or with other creatives. Whichever way you engage with your independent creative voice, remember it is curiosity that fuels your creativity. Be interested in the world around you, in what you do not know or understand, discover new information and ideas and your creativity will thrive. Spend time considering how you see the world on a local, national and global level. What would you change? Even a microcosmic change engages you in the act of considering a wider view and of dreaming up solutions. In turn this helps you to develop your authentic voice. How could you be proactive and help to make the change you envision through your art?

An actor who chooses not to engage actively in the creation of art and exists only to service other creatives can easily become a puppet. There is no creative endeavour for you to explore if you are entirely controlled. As an independent actor, you take permission to engage in shaping the art and the right to influence its direction of travel. You are not a puppet; your creative contribution is unique, important, and vital. We must also understand that not every creative venture is run as an artistic cooperative or has months of experimentation afforded it where actors have an equal input. To that end, the actor may give a more measured artistic input to positively achieve the collective goals within the time frame. Whilst hierarchical working rarely makes for exciting results artistically, adhering to structures and parameters can positively fuel creativity. The actor as creative artist is not there to do the job of the director, but they do have an equally important and different role in realising the finished work.

It can feel difficult to maintain creativity if you are pursuing a self-led approach to training or when you are not working on an acting contract. If you do not feel creative, you will not trust your instinct or feel confident. This can mean a negative spiral begins where you do not take your creativity seriously because of a loss of confidence. The importance of keeping your creative resource topped up cannot be overstated. Particularly in quieter periods, you can be actively creative rather than waiting for others to validate your artistry. It is essential to feature creativity somewhere prominently in your scheduled week, to stay open and to maintain your artistic confidence. Curiosity, commitment and courage are once again key to enabling you as an intelligent, instinctive actor to not only interrogate your work and grow, but also to flourish creatively.

The list of activities that can help to exercise your creativity is endless and must be steered by your own curiosity. Cultural stimuli are often useful in offering new perspectives and igniting your imagination – anything that differs from your everyday experience is good. Seeing, hearing, touching, smelling and living new experiences will awaken your imagination and can create connections and even epiphany moments. Live in the world – do not be lured into a hibernating world of streaming devices or games consoles. Excellent as these are in moderation for downtime and leisure, they can also act as an anaesthetic rather than an inspiration.

Exposing yourself to the world by leaving your front door takes effort but will always change your mindset and could spark new thoughts, feelings and ideas. Travel is a rich resource for the actor; it enables you to see new landscapes that can fire your imagination, to meet new people in different cultural settings and experience languages, dialects and food different from your own. The best actors celebrate difference and allow their curiosity to push them to explore unknown places.

We log all our experiences in the mind consciously or unconsciously and they form a library for the actor to draw upon. This library needs new additions and updates frequently to avoid it becoming dusty and irrelevant. Acting is action and so the act of engaging in action will improve your acting without you even trying. Try out crafts from crochet, basket weaving or mosaics – they will spur your artistry as will physical adventure. Try activities that put you out of your comfort zone; they can wake you up, encourage mindfulness and help to keep your creativity exercised. Exercising your imagination, your sense of invention and the creation of original connections is a very useful daily habit. To live fully as an artist and to immerse yourself in creativity is a joyful endeavour.

Looking for the conditions in which your creativity can flourish is important. You can direct your experiences to help foster your creative instinct, let other people inspire you and ignite your imagination or curate creative habits to make part of your week. Try choosing one suggestion from each of these groups that will help you to develop the ability to engage with your creativity; make sure to change your choices regularly and make sure creativity becomes your new habit.

Acting related

- watching films
- going to the theatre
- watching site-specific performance
- reading scripts
- attending acting skills classes
- learning some text
- writing your own work.

Arts related

- go to a museum
- go to a gallery
- go to an art exhibition
- go to a photography exhibition
- go to the opera
- go to a ballet or dance performance
- listen to radio drama and podcasts.

Creative skills

- write poetry, spoken word, rap, songs, short stories
- paint and draw
- learn sculpting or pottery
- play a musical instrument
- practise photography
- crochet, knit, macramé
- sew and use textiles.

Experiences

- moving meditation
- people watching

- daydreaming
- travel – local, national, international
- cooking and inventing new recipes
- adventure and adrenalin activities
- meeting new people.

Your journal gives you space to record your experience of the activities you engage in. Focus on the experience, the feelings and thoughts evoked, rather than writing descriptive passages about what you did. Experiment using colour in your life, in your clothes, your home environment and the spaces you visit. Colour stimulates our thoughts, and ideas. There is no right or wrong way to exercise your creativity, your aim is to stay tuned in to your instincts and let them guide you.

Dreaming

Dream at every opportunity you can. Night- and daydreaming are good for you, they help the mind in its processing. You can also dream by focussing on your goals and visualising them and this is great for confidence building. Daydreaming is probably the most joy filled of your dreaming options and a valuable tool. Do you remember at school when the teacher reprimanded you or someone in your class for daydreaming? Whilst you will want to avoid doing it at work or when you are engaged in other activities, daydreaming is not a waste of time.

It is easy to assume that the daydreamer is lazy, reneging on their responsibilities and not paying attention. In fact, this slightly meditative state is one of deep attention where conscious and unconscious thoughts merge. Periods of daydreaming enhance our creativity; they act in a percolating way, providing a channel for the imagination (see Imagination). This can enable us to make new associations, explore new ideas or possibilities and filter what we know, without controlling these thoughts. Regardless of what the daydream is based on, it is a useful tool for filtering your ideas. Daydreaming has no negative consequences, and it can liberate the imagination, helping it to make bold leaps.

Often considered as an indulgent activity, daydreaming for the actor is a necessity and a wonderful tool for making sense of abstract ideas and ethereal connections, and letting preparation or information settle. It can be an incredibly constructive activity. You will need to give yourself permission to daydream – no one else will – and allow yourself to be somewhere comfortable where you will not be distracted. Ideally, position yourself somewhere with an expansive horizon, looking through a window or sitting on the grass. Instead, you may prefer to daydream with your eyes closed.

Refrain from placing a time restraint on your daydreaming – do not try to control it. If you struggle to drift off, it can help to begin by visualising a goal you wish to achieve and seeing yourself successfully fulfilling it. This can kick-start your imagination by giving it a clear target to begin with; from there it can meander to a free stream of consciousness. When you come round after a period of daydreaming, it can feel as if you have taken a short nap and you may experience a sense of peace and restfulness.

Practising daydreaming will equip you to practise creative immersion. This happens when you place focus on a creative activity and lose sense of time and space. You are conscious and active but entirely absorbed in your world. Many people refer to it as being in the 'zone'. Creative immersion is not purely a state of concentration though; by following your imaginative instincts you begin channelling and expressing yourself as you become absorbed. Immersion comes with practice as it has more control than a dream state and can only really happen when you feel safe enough in your environment or company to relinquish any conscious hold on your reality as you create.

Multi-hyphenate artists

The actor as a singular identity needing to hide other skills, ambitions or pathways in their portfolio was a purist ideology which pervaded the twentieth century. The system was suspicious of actors who also referred to themselves as directors or producers or writers for example; these skills were separated and hidden to a degree. Such notions of the actor as a singular artist are oppressive, trapping the actor, reducing their place in the creative hierarchy, restricting them from further creative exploration. The skills and aptitudes of most actors are not constrained to acting, even though they may choose to give it a singular focus. Many actors are polymaths: creatives who excel in more than one area and are better served if they celebrate the 'hyphenation' of these skills. The rise of acceptance for multi-hyphenate artists is a welcome change and the days of reducing résumés to appear less creatively 'threatening' thankfully gone. Old attitudes are changing and will now disappear with time.

British actor–playwright–director–singer–broadcaster–artistic director Kwame Kwei-Armah OBE was one of the first voices in the arts to celebrate multi-hyphenated artists:

> I find myself interested in the multidisciplinary artist, the slash artist [...] I'm interested in flying the flag for them, saying this is going to be a place for you, you don't need to hide your multiple dimensions [...] I think we are living in a different time, there isn't a theatre maker under thirty describing themselves in singular terms. We all know we're going to have to have multiple jobs in our careers to live, and I think now artists have come to the fore, they can be 3 or 4 things [...] I'm really interested in what being a hyphenated artist means to the world and to the way you see the world.
>
> Kwame Kwei-Armah, BBC Sounds, Behind the Scenes, 10 October 2018. https://www.bbc.co.uk/sounds/play/m0000ndr (Accessed 26 August 2023)

Creativity is not limited, those artists who are critical of the multi-hyphenates tend to be so out of fear – for their own employment, for comparison to their own skillset, for change. The expansion of possibilities for the actor to multi-hyphenate their creative offer is also a way of future-proofing careers. Following the pandemic, global instability, and a radical shift in opportunities in the arts, future-proofing has never been more important. Actors have always needed additional income and, now this stigma is dissolving, they can diversify and rightly celebrate their talents, helping both to pay their rent and to develop creatively.

This celebration of the multi-hyphenate artist is possible largely thanks to generation Y – the so-called 'Millennials'. Their desire to embrace change and a healthy disinterest in rules generally give them a lack of deference to the establishment and that has changed the landscape of opportunity. Generation Z are now living in an arts culture that has normalised this change. I am proud of so many of my graduates who are now openly balancing successful portfolio careers as multi-hyphenate artists: actor–writer–director–producer–vlogger–music artist–theatre-maker–presenter–facilitator–comedian–activist–teacher–agent. To become a multi-hyphenate artist you must take a decision to widely develop your skills and actively say *yes* to opportunities; this will allow an organic set of hyphens to develop from your own curiosity. A composite or portfolio career helps you in developing artistic insight, interdisciplinary insight, and in making original connections (see Imagination).

CHAPTER FOUR

Process

Process is the set of actions we engage with when pursuing our performance goals and the way in which we choose to approach the work. It encompasses preparation, rehearsal, performance and reflection. As you develop throughout your career, you will adjust your process as you gain fuller understanding of how you work, your creative input and how you can best deliver from project to project. Some actors may tell you they have no process – this is usually a sign of experience rather than a literal truth, with the actor having embedded a process of which they are no longer conscious.

Each phase of the performance process is unique and requires different tasks from the actor. Your skills practice helps you to know your strengths and challenges and this self-knowledge will help you dictate the way in which you approach your process. Never put the onus on the director, other creatives or actors to dictate your process; own your part in the creative venture. You are responsible for what you deliver, and the process is the opportunity you have waited for; indulge your creativity as an artist, liberate yourself and take your space. If you accept new learning and capture it for future use, it will serve you forever. Sometimes a project will lack any meaningful collaboration, such as a commercial venture that is time strapped. These experiences require you to entirely own your process.

Your process needs to be quick to adapt as demands can vary substantially between theatre, screen work and voice recorded media. In theatre, each of the team engages in a personal process and the full company engages in a collective process led by their director. Never rely on the collective process in the room to be a substitute for your own work; the collective process places focus on the production, creative vision and collaboration. To be fully open to that process you will need to have engaged and be engaging with your own acting process independently. Every part of your process gives you the opportunity to consolidate and to refine your choices – use your journal to keep track of them.

By separating each stage of the process, it is easier to understand the shape of the trajectory you are embarking on. The shape below is a common one for theatre but by no means a blueprint. You can see that preparation is a key feature of the entire process. Theatre is live and so the demand on ensuring the work is secure before meeting an audience is strong. Commercial projects can reduce rehearsals down to 1, 2 or 3 weeks and in these instances, treat your preparation as you do for filming.

Process												
Week	**−1**	**−2**	**−3**	**−4**	**1**	**2**	**3**	**4**	**+1**	**+2**	**+3**	**+4**	**+5 onwards**
	Preparation				Preparation				Technical preparation				Performance preparation
					Rehearsals				Previews				Performance

On film sets, expect to deliver without any collaborative process to nurture you. Whilst you can learn a good deal from those on set with you and of course take direction as given, you will have consolidated your choices, completed your own preparation and be ready to shoot as per the filming schedule. Likewise, for recorded voice work, you will need to be prepared to work in the moment and without collaboration, albeit your producer will guide your choices when necessary.

Preparation

Preparation, whatever you consider that to be, is not optional. It is the starting point of your process and if carefully considered will bring you confidence and a sense of security that allows you to take artistic risks. If you care about the goal of performance, you must prepare for it at each stage. Day one of rehearsals is not the start of the process, the preparation phase is. During preparation, you set up the groundwork for being able to make informed artistic choices. Some of these choices you can consider in preparation and trial through experiment in rehearsals, others you will only discover through the actual experience of working in performance.

Text analysis, research, character work, accent breakdown, memorisation using mind and body, physical and vocal skills acquisition, repetition, fitness and wellbeing – all of this is preparation. Preparation is not the enemy of spontaneity (see Imagination), you prepare in order to be free, spontaneous and risk-taking. Preparation is the opportunity to dig beneath the surface of the material or concept you are working with and identify unique connections. Most preparation happens alone and at the beginning of the process; it usually includes the more cerebral work, requiring you to absorb new knowledge and understanding. Only once you have done this can you really identify what practical preparation is required.

There are exceptions to every rule – you will meet actors who apparently do not prepare, never warm up and seemingly nail every job they get. Experience as an actor can change your early habits and there is more than one way of engaging in preparation. However, starting from a position of being super prepared can only ever work in your favour and support your confidence.

Depending on the project, you will usually start your preparation with the work you can do on and around the script, considering the production concept. If the setting of the production is relocated to Argentina from Scotland there is little point in focussing on Scottish research! The production concept is always key in informing and steering your preparation. If the director is choosing to retell *Hamlet* from Ophelia's perspective, this will inform your choice of background work – often termed as the 'invisible work' it hides from view.

By deconstructing the script, understanding plot, character, relationships and events (see Text and Character), you start to immerse yourself in the world of the action. You will uncover what you do not know about the world in which it is set, character-specific information will surface, so make sure to take notes and remember to return to these specifics. There are likely to be words you are unfamiliar with too, so write them down and look up the meaning and pronunciation – do not wait for rehearsals to bluff your way through it.

Your work on the script and your understanding of the production concept then determine your associated research. It may include historical reading for factual accuracy, listening to targeted podcasts, seeking images to create a visual understanding, viewing film footage that illuminates content, style or background and so on (see Context). Research can send you down rabbit holes and whilst you can discover interesting new knowledge, remember, there is infinite knowledge available, and you need to be selective in curating it. You can always return to other sources if you need to.

There may not be a script if the work is experimental, movement led or devised but there will still be contextual research you can engage in, such as around the starting point or concept. This research enables you to begin rehearsals with some resources to share with the company and can help you to bond. Keeping a clear list of your sources so you could return to them really does help. Imagine you are a detective – your preparation is an investigation where you are looking for clues and assembling facts. As you discover leads and research them, new questions will evolve; research should always throw up more questions than it resolves (see Context). Try to ignore your assumptions and avoid researching simply to prove yourself right, it will narrow your perspective and make it difficult to see other options. Keep a list of the questions you generate and use it as a template to guide your natural curiosity.

Much of your focus may be character related and a character specific list will help you distinguish this element from the wider contextual research. In naturalistic plays, a key area to investigate is the active life of the character (see Character) such as occupation, hobbies and skills. It is common to need to learn new skills to accurately play the part and generate artistic choices. For example, if your character is a chess champion, you need to have at least a practical working understanding of how to play chess. Indeed, once you have learnt these skills for a role, they can stay with you and boost your own creativity (see Creativity). Knitting, touch typing, horse-riding, drumming, juggling, cocktail mixing, speaking Spanish, flower arranging, making protest banners, yodelling – the list is endless.

Preparation need not be time intensive or arduous; in fact, it is usually incredibly fulfilling and even exciting! The golden rule is to be organised – identify your goals and schedule realistic time for achieving them within your time frame. Each different project will require its own bespoke focus and needs – this may be due to its medium, its scale, its style or your own personal context. Never allow preparation to be dutiful, do it because it will help you; no one is watching, there is no one to please but yourself.

> On day one of preparation, identify the following:
>
> - What you need to do – write a list.
> - The order in which you need to do it – draw a diagram.
> - The areas which are new to you or scare you most – prioritise them.
> - Create a plan which you can refer to and change as necessary.

The preparation period can be the countdown towards rehearsals or to performance and the length of it will depend on when you are contracted in relation to the production schedule commencing. Most actors will want to immerse themselves in preparation with a lead in time of at least four weeks, but it really depends on what time you have available. Busy actors moving between contracts may sometimes have days to prepare rather than weeks. Equally, you may have six months. Whatever time you have available, make the most of it by consciously deciding how much you want to use of the time you have. Several elements of your preparation can be worked on simultaneously, so you make immediate connections rather than isolating elements to then connect them.

By being in control you can then actually allow the preparation time to *prepare* you, and this will mean you can remain in the moment once you are in rehearsals or performance.

Preparation			
Week –4	Week –3	Week –2	Week –1
Acquiring new essential skills			
Timelines, research and analysis		Units, objectives, actions, thoughts	
Physical, vocal and emotional experimentation			
Accent breakdown and line memorisation			

Learning lines

One thing is for certain, if there are lines with your name on them, you need to learn them unless you are working in a sound booth or using an autocue or teleprompter. It is an important part of the job and complaining about it will never relieve the need to do it – so embrace it. Even if the director has not been specific about a time frame for line learning (being 'off book'), it is inevitable and will need to happen eventually. Getting the text memorised as soon as possible enables you to embed it sooner. Even if you are working with a director who spends a good deal of time engaging in 'table work' on the script, you are at no disadvantage by already knowing your lines. Just be sure you do not fix the delivery of your lines at this stage.

For as long as you are an actor, people will ask you '*how did you learn all those lines?*' So, get an answer. Indeed, you would prefer questions about your emotional connection to the character or your wonderful stage presence, but these questions will feature far less often. By finding an answer to the line-learning question, you are taking ownership of the subject and you will be able to deal with it. So how *do* you learn your lines?

If you struggle in isolation memorising lines from the page, change your approach. Even visual learners sometimes struggle to learn in this way and find that creating associated images to the words helps them to remember and to link sections. Other actors record their lines and playback to themselves or record the feed lines and then pause to speak their lines. Asking your 'acting buddy', family or friends to read in or test you can also help. If you learn kinaesthetically, engage in an activity – sweeping the floor or planting in the garden to assimilate the text through motion. On the other hand, perhaps you have a photographic memory enabling you to retain a picture of the lines on the page, which is a huge advantage unless the script changes.

Whichever method you have used to learn your lines, it is also a good idea to complete a layer of practice that is physical. Once you think you have all your lines learnt, find a good-sized space – garden, park, beach are ideal – and speak all your lines whilst moving continuously, skipping, sprinting, dancing or rolling down a hill.

Keep the motion continuous and not only will you find some joy, you will get the text into your body and ready to work with. Learn your text accurately, including punctuation, and do not paraphrase. The writer has deliberately constructed each word in their written order, changing any of them changes intention, meaning, style or scansion (see Text). This is essential for theatre but film or television work can often be more forgiving and can present an opposite test, giving you licence to paraphrase (see Text).

During your preparation, right or wrong does not exist in terms of creative choices, though there are some technical elements within the preparation period which *are* right or wrong. For example, line learning, music learning or specific accent or dialect work. It is a good idea to nail these first, so you understand the parameters you are working within. During the preparation process, you are using these absolutes as parameters to inform your choices. The theatre medium gives you the most space for trial and error, enabling you to prepare for a rehearsal period in addition to preparing for performance. Your preparation in theatre work continues throughout rehearsals and into the run of a production; it is not a discrete element of the process. However, by the first rehearsal you should feel confident about the following:

- Who the creative team and actors are

- You have visited the venue to see a production in the space (if possible)

- Understanding plot, sub-plots and structure of the material

- Understanding who your character is in the context of the play and their relationships

- Knowledge of references in the text that are historical or unfamiliar to you, including words you have not previously encountered

- Understanding stage directions and their impact

- Characterisation – your analysis and your practical work

- Being ready to try out choices and work with direction.

Screen work

This invariably cuts to the chase and expects you to turn up on set ready to deliver. Preparation must be complete prior to the shoot and you will need to be ready to give the director a finished offering based on their brief to you. This independence can be daunting at first but if you focus well on your preparation, you have nothing to fear. Filming is inordinately expensive and whilst the performance is not live for an audience, the environment is live for the actor and crew. To this end, it is helpful to see it as live performance rather than a rehearsal setting where repeats are possible.

Some directors do run a form of rehearsal, but time is money, and you should expect to arrive already on point and be quick to adapt to direction. Filming out of sequence is standard practice and can be due to location groupings, availabilities and daylight needs. It is essential in your preparation for you to know the character timeline and journey in its chronological form so you can commit to emotional and psychological choices out of sequence. The nature of recording is that the final product is committed and only changeable by edit, which is not in the actor's gift. It is a great aspiration to want to nail the first take and it will make you popular.

If screen work is new to you, a short course to understand camera shots and angles, hitting your mark, continuity and how it works will be very useful. It is the medium that is different, not you. In terms of acting, you will require the same tools as you do for all your work. The ongoing rapid development of new technology also opens out new possibilities. Computer Generated Imagery (CGI) means the actor's imagination on set is even more important than usual. You may have dialogue with an absent animated character or be at the centre of a furious battle with dinosaurs or have all manner of death and destruction sweeping past you. Know the scenario, your text, be alive in your senses and understand the emotional impact and the stakes of the scene. Beyond that your work will be helped by green screen, motion capture and direction. CGI has reduced the need for actors or stunt people to perform all the dangerous action in a film. Motion Capture relies on your movement skills and this work can help to generate animated characters. A short course to gain the opportunity to work with this equipment is a good idea if you can.

Audio recording

For voiceovers, radio drama, audiobooks, animation or voiced gaming contracts, you are required to adhere to the studio timetable by delivering as efficiently as possible – once again time is money. There is rarely much rehearsal to speak of; in many instances, it will be your first engagement with the script and you will be delivering for a producer. Many actors now work from a home set-up – a recording booth in their home or garage, which may relieve a small degree of pressure but remains time sensitive.

Prepare for this work by ensuring a thorough voice and physical warm-up. Your ability to deliver on time and with great results will heavily influence your future contracts. Even though your audience cannot see you, being in your body is essential. You will be more creative mentally and your voice will be at its peak if your body is released, relaxed and energised. Practise your sight-reading aloud every day – articulate words, make sense of the line and effortlessly characterise your lines by engaging intonation, pitch and range.

Rehearsal

Rehearsal is distinct from your own pre-rehearsal preparation. It is the opportunity to bring all your preparation into the studio and work confidently with the other actors and the creative team. Rehearsal is the opportunity to play, to create, to collaborate and be guided on your choices. If you have prepared well then you will be free to play, if you have not, you will be bluffing and stuck between adrenalin and fear – feeling lost (see Wellbeing). It is entirely in your gift to be well prepared and be able to enjoy the process of rehearsal. Be confident and ensure your nerves do not push you into sabotaging your best efforts. Assumptions based on previous experience of rehearsals are dangerous and can close you to new experiences. Allow the rehearsal period to be new and unique and without comparison so it can reveal itself to you as you experience it. Avoid any secrecy in the rehearsal room and bring an open and kind energy.

Rehearsal rooms are like busy hives. There are many unseen pressures and there are deadlines the actors may not know about.

The Deputy Stage Manager (DSM) is the key person for you to report to in terms of any practical issues. Try to avoid going through the creative team for practical logistics – the DSM will communicate with the company manager and others when they need to know. There are many accepted ways of being in the rehearsal room that you are well advised to commit to. It is a unique environment, and these invisible rules exist to enable the company in the space to stay focussed and for the space to be as safe as is possible and creative. Rehearsals can become highly pressurised, and everyone has a responsibility to maintain the equilibrium so creativity can thrive:

- Be a bright, calm, positive, sociable and a respected company member
- Be early and then ready to start on time – check the call sheet carefully
- Wear clothes you can do your best work in
- Do a vocal/physical warm-up
- Turn off your mobile phone and other devices
- Have the entire script and a pencil with an eraser
- Have a notebook and pen or tablet to write notes
- Rehearsal is not for learning lines – know your lines as required
- Actively watch and give your energy to the rehearsal in progress if you are in the room
- Contribute to the group or focus and be silent when necessary
- Give a supportive, generous energy, be inspired by fellow actors
- Avoid clock watching
- Avoid eating and drinking unless this culture is encouraged
- Avoid audio recording or filming rehearsal unless asked to
- Let your director evaluate the work

- Respect the writer's work

- Immerse yourself

- Never make excuses, just make offers

- Be bold and make 'mistakes'

- Take responsibility for your part

- Retain work from previous rehearsals

- Develop and fix director notes prior to rehearsal

- Enjoy the challenge of problem solving.

Director's notes are professional and not personal – intended to develop your offers, they are essential to the progression of the work. Always remember that the director can see the whole stage picture and has had conversations with the production team of which you will be unaware. Be ready with your notebook or tablet, script, pen and pencil and write down every note you receive. Listen carefully but never try to just remember them – record them accurately. Notes can sometimes encourage you to think more deeply in an area, so take your time to process this feedback. Allow the director to finish giving notes before discussing a particular note with them and avoid asking for endless explanation following a notes session. Take the notes, work them and bring back new offers – be independent.

Even if the director is happy with your work, continue your pursuit; they are not a guru and they do not have all the answers.

Guided by the director or creative team you will be a part of the bigger picture – the production – and this to varying degrees will involve a group process led by the director. Some directors pay no attention at all to this, and others immerse entirely in a group process. One of the main reasons I espouse a magpie approach to actor training is the need for you to be flexible enough to work unfazed with a range of different directors with different approaches. Being open and ready to explore your work through the prism of the director's approach, enables you to use the elements of your work that are most effective, whilst being part of a collective working process.

The first day of rehearsals can feel like the first day of school: fears that you will know less and have less to contribute than anyone else or be less good or less experienced. Shyness around being in a new room full of new people is also common and may cause anxiety – this is entirely normal and exciting; remember to breathe and sit with it (see Wellbeing). The full company assembles for the first day of theatre rehearsals and this may be the only time you are with some of the production team, so enjoy their company.

Rehearsal lengths can differ in theatre from as little as a week in weekly rep (now almost extinct) to long and less defined periods of development. Longer rehearsals cost more but can prioritise the integrity of the work and its needs. In the bigger subsidised houses in the UK and in the USA on Broadway, you will usually get up to six weeks and then run previews. On average in the UK and USA, most rehearsal periods span three to four weeks followed by technical rehearsals and previews before opening. Press night is the trigger for moving into the performance run. At this point, stage management take over the running of the show, the director moves on to a new project and an assistant director then usually supports the company.

In other parts of Europe, there are instances of rehearsing for months in pursuit of truth. Elsewhere, in Southeast Asia there is a stock repertoire of performances that actors learn and are engaged to revive and so rehearsal becomes recap. The length of rehearsals anywhere in the world will depend on financial considerations, what the production needs and the availability of creatives. For example, new written work may benefit from a longer rehearsal period with the writer present, following a research and development phase (R&D).

Rehearsals usually work on a scheduled call system with members of the company called at different times for rehearsals dependent on their track. Make sure you read the call sheet carefully; calls may be specific to you, such as a costume fitting, scene work, fight call, intimacy call, or be full company calls, so check thoroughly. Schedules are complex and take in a raft of availability factors, artistic and access needs, so unless your agent has negotiated time out of rehearsals for you, the expectation is that you will be fully available on every working day. Whilst you may know the overarching rehearsal plan, the final call sheet may not come until the night before and will often be a surprise. It is important that the team can schedule fluidly – in theatre you are preparing for a live event so deadlines are fixed, and the team need to be reactive to the schedule as rehearsals progress.

The rehearsal space will be 'marked up' by the stage management team to represent the exact dimensions of the stage space. This allows you to be accurate in moving through the playing space, understanding the exact positions of entrances and exits, levels, set furniture and audience. Take time to study the mark-up so you can be as effective in the space as possible. It will give you a shorthand with the creative team who have spent weeks and months in advance of rehearsals planning every inch of the space and its configuration (see Space). If you are touring with the production, the mark-up becomes even more precious in rehearsals as it can be disorienting moving into theatre spaces with different architectural designs and slightly different audience configurations. The sense of space created by the height of the auditorium affects the actor and therefore their relationship with their audience (see Space).

Preparation continues throughout the rehearsal period when you will be preparing for rehearsals by processing new work from rehearsals to date, consolidating lines, and practising any technical work such as choreography, stage fighting or intimacy. It can also help to find time with your scene partners outside of the rehearsal room to discuss or work specific moments. This preparation happens when you have no calls in rehearsals or outside of the working week.

Preparation for rehearsals is also about warming up. The warm-up should be specific for your needs and be dictated by the demands of the work and the content of your calls on any specific day. For example, a singing call will require different preparation than table work. Warming up is both a safety preparation and an opportunity to release so you can optimise your freedom in rehearsals. A warm voice or body will have more flexibility and dexterity and a warm imagination will fuel the level of joy and creative energy you bring to the room. There may be a designated company warm-up and this can be a fantastic communal preparation encouraging bonding and imaginative connection.

Every actor is different, from their metabolism to stamina, experience, skill level and injury history. So, in addition to any group warm-up, ensure you also focus some time on yourself. Know what you need and facilitate it prior to your call. You can tailor your personal warm-up using your knowledge of the challenges you face in your practice. If you struggle with vocal clarity, then spend time on articulation exercises; if you have a long-standing injury, use the exercises you know will help you safely release tension in this area. If you are not a morning person, you may need to wake up your brain and emotional facility more than other actors do. Yoga to music can help to wake you up with stretching and creative stimulation. Alternatively, you may simply drink black coffee and complete a Sudoku – it really is your choice. There are no rules but a warm-up will always put you in a better place to deliver your best work.

Healthy ingredients for an independent personal warm-up:

- Breathing – semi-supine (on your back with knees raised and feet on floor) floor release.
- Energetic connection – energy activating tapping and shaking.
- Physical release – from spine rolls to freestyle spontaneous movement.
- Cardio – short intense bursts of running, skipping, lifting and resistance.
- Coordination – moving and speaking, dancing and singing, juggling.
- Agility and dexterity – balance, jumps, obstacle course.
- Voicing sounds – humming, sirens, natural sound responses to action.
- Articulation – repetition of fricatives, glottal stops and consonant endings.
- Play – hula hoop, ball in a hoop, silent disco (if in company).
- Text – speed run lines whilst throwing a ball to the wall or singing.

Rehearsals take a myriad of shapes, depending on factors including: the material, the production concept, the creative team, the intended audience, the location, the rehearsal space, the cast and levels of experience within the company. The list is endless because it is a creative process and the content imagined prior to rehearsals can shift and change shape relative to the people in the room and the ideas that evolve. Rehearsal practices across the world have their own traditions and the nature of creative practice means they evolve over time or through influence – there are no definitive descriptions.

At the first company meeting there will usually be a meet and greet and often a first read-through. The production concept and design may be shared, company administration and a sharing of the direction of artistic travel. Remember that the creative team will have been working independently of the cast in decision making around style, set, costume and props. Be careful to remain open to all new information that will feed the work you have already prepared. There are five main phases of rehearsal and, although they differ in length or are sometimes conflated, they will usually occur in some form in most rehearsal processes:

1 Exploration

This is the initial opportunity to explore the themes, content, message or style of the piece. It can involve workshopping ideas through movement, visual stimuli, improvisation and sound. It may involve masks, puppets or technical experiments with light and shadow, video or virtual reality. The exploration phase may encompass accumulated research as a stimulus and begin the process of sharing company knowledge (see Context and Creativity). This phase may usually last anywhere from a day to two weeks.

2 Collective understanding

This can happen before the exploration phase, after it or alongside it. It may include multiple read-throughs. If the company is working from a text then this is the opportunity to agree an understanding of meaning, share textual analysis and plant roots for the dramatic shape of the work. You may also share understanding of research and open any unanswered questions so far (see Context and Text).

At this point, the company is building a common vocabulary that will serve them in the next phase of work.

3 Staging

This is the opportunity to work through the entire script in sections, making choices about where characters are in the space – blocking – and the shape and mechanics of each scene physically. It is usual to divide the work on the script into units, scenes or events depending on the working process of the director. It is then possible to approach these sections chronologically or out of sequence. You may draw on work explored earlier in the process and find a home for it or be informed by its results. The actor is on the move with their script and pencil as they work with the director, this phase deals with practicalities alongside artistic discoveries. Once a first sketch of the staging is complete, the director may return in detail to the whole work and colour it in or move on to a 'stagger through' before they go back. Once sketched in, it is common to revisit the first and the last scenes the most.

Some directors will choreograph their blocking in advance of rehearsals and the actors will learn it like a sequence. The challenge for the actor involved in this working method is to find purpose for the physical track – like dance, they must understand *why* the character moves where it does and *how* it does. Piecing together a through line of movement is essential to emotional connection and playing intentions. When taking direction, translate the director's notes into a language that enables you to deliver, by figuring out the journey to it yourself. This counts too for choreographers, musical directors and movement directors who may not always speak an actor's language.

During the staging period and towards the end of it, the team will increasingly consider their audience. What will be the audience reception of the production concept? Will its meaning be realised? Does the comedic or dramatic build of the work have the desired impact? Each of these questions and others will inform the ongoing tweaks and changes to the work. You must continue to stay independently focussed on your own role to achieve your very best work.

4 Runs

This phase is the opportunity for the full company to experience how the whole piece fits together. The first run in the rehearsal room or 'stagger through' reveals how well the story is being told, which moments are working well, what areas require the most work and what needs to be changed. It will usually be 'off book' as far as is possible and this is a pivotal moment in the rehearsal journey. Depending on how the work is structured whether written or devised, it may be contained in a single act or have multiple acts (see Text). This will dictate whether the subsequent runs will cover the entire work or be broken up. It is common with a written play in two acts for a director to return to work in detail on an act and run it in isolation before piecing it all back together.

If the style of work utilises direct address with the audience, runs can incorporate the cast or production team as an audience to rehearse the interaction. Runs are a great opportunity for you to embed all the work you have assimilated. Only once this work is fully embedded can you be free to play. This later stage of the rehearsal period provides you with the opportunity to consolidate everything so far and to be reactive to new cuts to lines or action. If cutting impacts on your lines, do not take it personally, it really has nothing to do with you and everything to do with making the production as good as possible. Runs are also the opportunity for the production team to review risk assessments and ensure the production is ready for the technical and dress rehearsal phase.

The only limiting factor on the number of runs in the rehearsal room is the schedule. Regardless of the number of runs scheduled, if rehearsals have unexpectedly needed to place more focus on a particular area, these may be reduced. It is important to be as ready and as independent as possible; if runs are cut you do not want to feel overly anxious. Use each run for a different purpose; explore a different aspect of your work such as emotional connection or your relationship to another character. This may be steered by the director but be ready to set yourself personal goals. Use the last rehearsal in the room to boost your confidence and celebrate the company.

Most productions will not move from the rehearsal space to the performance space until they are ready to begin 'tech'. The 'get in' is led by the technical crew of the production team and occurs before actors are scheduled to arrive. The whole team is then immersed in the installing of set, scenic painting, audience seating configuration, rigging of lights, sound and projection, focus for lights, sound check and dressing room set up. All of this happens before the process of tech can begin. The lighting and sound plot cues are then programmed and the full company including actors is ready to assemble.

Technical rehearsals can be disorienting, you will be in a new space in a darkened setting surrounded by a team on 'cans' who know more than you do about what is happening. This can be the most wonderful opportunity to practise being in the moment and enjoying the chance to relinquish some pressure from yourself. Tech involves a lot of waiting and a lot of repetition. Use this to acclimatise with the space and exits, working through your track with the specificity of light and sound brings a new chance to hone your precision and timing (see Space).

Patience is a wonderful virtue in the context of a technical rehearsal. Remember that for the technical team it is their first rehearsal. Being patient and kind will enable them to do their best job, respect them and treat them as your equals, which they are. Tech also requires that you listen intently, so you are ready to take instruction from the Production or Stage Manager as quickly as possible. If asked to stand in a specific position, be still and remain there until given the go ahead to move. Likewise, if asked to speak to test a microphone, keep speaking until told otherwise.

The technical rehearsal is the first opportunity in the space to run 'stage business' with elements such as liquids, food, fake blood, fake firearms. It is important that you have a good level of focus, so time is not wasted. Each of these moments is repeated until they work artistically and until they are deemed safe. Haze, smoke, dry ice, confetti drops and pyrotechnics can all be difficult to get used to, but remember that the audience is becoming increasingly central to the production goals at this point and these effects can be crucial. Technical rehearsal is not the time to try out new blocking, alter physical action or paraphrase – the entire theatre is relying on you to be reliable. Trust in what has been rehearsed and stick with it. There will be space for newness once you know the parameters and you are in the performance part of the process.

In these final stages of rehearsal, you will need to prepare psychologically for an audience. Take your time to stand in the playing space and imagine their positioning (see Space). If you have any direct address to the audience, try it out on any production team members if they are in the auditorium. Allow yourself to meet their eyes and to connect, this will make your first preview a lot easier and help you to manage your adrenalin effectively.

The technical run stops and starts at plotted cues or during moments of action that require technical rehearsal. It includes all production elements with the cast fully costumed with hair and make-up and wigs as required. This enables the full team to assess any solutions required to achieve the aesthetic or dramatic goals, to rehearse unusual entrances or exits and to work through the timing of quick changes. It is difficult to predict the length of a technical run, it depends entirely on the production – its length, complexity, what has been solved in the rehearsal room and who the individual members of the company and production team are. The technical rehearsal period can be long, slow and seemingly without end. Do your part in keeping company spirits high – the atmosphere can be tense, so bringing a calm yet excited energy will help those around you.

At the end of the 'tech' all cues will have been confirmed and stage business will be working to the satisfaction of the director. There are usually two dress rehearsals, and these present an opportunity to focus attention on costume, both from an aesthetic perspective and a practical one. If the actor is more restricted in their dancing or their hat is impeding them from a particular action, the designer and wardrobe team will fix it. Unless you are asked for your opinion on the look of your costume, do not offer it. You cannot see the finished effect onstage under lights or in relation to the set and other costumes. You must trust that other experts are making good choices for good reasons.

Dress rehearsals may have select guests of the producers watching and can be a great opportunity for you. Your primary focus must be to use it as a final opportunity to hone your choices, make sense of your through line, to be entirely sure of all changes made during the technical process and to play. Whether you are preparing for the first preview or whether you are in a fringe show where opening night doubles as press night and there are no previews, you are now preparing for an audience to share the experience with you. Each of these five phases of rehearsals requires your independent focus, your company spirit and your belief in the work. Once you have completed this part of the process you move into the performance phase.

5 Performance

Performance is the most compelling reason for actors wanting to do their job – the opportunity to share stories with an audience and to be witnessed; to give a voice to important subject matter, reflect on the human condition or to entertain and give pleasure. Whichever way you imagine your role as an actor, performance is your opportunity to realise it and share it.

If you are lucky enough to have previews, not only you but also the director and creative team will have an opportunity to review the work in front of an audience. This is the opportunity to test the production before the press make their judgement. It is very usual to make cuts in the material during previews and this can involve you learning new material, relearning sections, changing blocking or exits and needing to make new connections at speed due to cuts. This should not come as a surprise; it is a normal part of the process. Make the most of your time with the director during previews – it may be your last chance to work with them.

In the same way that you need to warm up for rehearsals you will need to warm up for performances. By now, you will know what you need specifically to prepare for this production. Organise your time so you can prepare effectively and do not be swayed by other actors who may not feel the need to warm themselves up – be independent. You may also feel the need to add calming elements to your warm-up if your response to adrenalin creates anxiety (see Wellbeing). Never use the first fifteen minutes of a show to warm up in front of your audience, this is a sloppy habit and is annoyingly common. The audience deserve all your energy, integrity, and expertise from curtain up.

Once you arrive at press night you will need to feel ready to hear the responses of the press and public. Even if you choose not to read these 'crits', someone else surely will and you are unlikely to escape them. Stay grounded, nothing on earth can please everyone and the noble effort of all creative endeavour is a cause for celebration.

Remember, the performance is not about you, it is about the story, themes and central ideas in the production. The actors, creative team, and *mise en scène* share these with the audience in a live setting and audience responses are immediate in the moment of creation. With screen and recorded voice work the audience will receive it relative to their own lives. The narrative, its plot and structure, style, characters and ideas will always impact an audience in some way (see Text). Your performance may be a key element of the whole, but it does not exist outside of the whole. Even the reception of a one-person show will include writing, direction, choreography and production values beyond a single contribution.

There will be moments in your working life as an actor where you may have a low opinion of the work you are involved in. Sometimes this is related to the script, to the work of other actors, a disagreement with the director, production team, choice of venue, marketing, film edit or a host of other reasons. Get perspective. It is rare for the stakes to be so incredibly high that this will matter a month after the performance or release. Your ego can cling to some sense of personal injustice but in truth, it does not matter. Take some space, get perspective, then make notes in your journal that identify what went wrong and what lessons you will take away.

You have the power to reject future contracts with people or teams with whom you feel fundamentally incompatible. Look deeply into yourself and examine if your frustration is in fact fear (see Wellbeing). On many more occasions than you may expect, the work you have complained bitterly about will be a roaring success with audiences. Every actor has an anecdote of a production much loved by the public or the press and hated by the actors. Try to find the humility to accept this difference of opinion when you reflect on your experience.

If you are in a position of having to comment on a production that a fellow actor is in and you feel very critical of it, find ways to address it that are kind, non-blaming and positive. Be truthful but also put yourself in their place and be kind. Even simply saying 'well done' after an event is helpful. Productions take vast hours of an actor's time and emotional resources regardless of the result, so it is never disingenuous to congratulate someone for their effort or the effort of the production.

Once the run of performances has begun, review your eating and sleeping patterns so you can be free to enjoy time with the company after performances. A contract that crosses over can mean you are in rehearsal during the day and performing at night. Prepare in advance, ensure you have the stamina to manage these alongside each other (see Wellbeing). Each performance is different because it is unique to the time of day/week/month/year, the venue if touring, the individual contexts of those performing and those watching, the length of the run, the weather, the national context and the international context. The size and make-up of the audience will also change the performance because an audience influences those in it and, in turn, they influence the actors. Be alive to the myriad of differences between performances and allow them to keep your spontaneity live. Never assume that you know how a show will go – you will always be wrong.

Always strive to do your best work. In theatre, saving it for influential guests, a Saturday night crowd, friends, agents, press night or last night is a poor decision. People are paying good money for their tickets and will often have incurred a raft of other expenses to attend (hotels, meals and travel) – it is a job of work. In any case, you must never assume to know who is watching that quiet Wednesday matinee. Remember how much you have looked forward to being onstage and savour every minute of the time you have. Unlike recorded media, at each moment onstage you only have one chance to deliver your best performance.

Critical reflection is a positive process once you have a little distance from the work you are evaluating. Honest critical reflection is one of the most powerful tools the independent actor has in developing their practice. It enables you to consider your practical work and to analyse what went well and why. It also gives you the opportunity to understand what challenges you still face and to consider how you might approach those. Use your journal to record your feelings, observations and feedback and commit to reflecting on it. It can help you find closure on a piece of work and benefit your future process.

CHAPTER FIVE

Imagination

Make imagination a priority in your development; it forms the roots of your creative endeavours re-connecting you with your inner child. Acting is playing. As children, we instinctively know how to play, though typically, the time we spend in schools diminishes this instinct. Most education systems focus on curbing instinctive behaviour and promoting conformity; creating a set of rules to follow. This form of censorship on the young mind can begin to restrict the imagination and deter individual flair. The curiosity and delight experienced by a child as it encounters life is what every actor is searching for – capturing innocence in truth.

The late educator Ken Robinson spent his career celebrating the power of the imagination and challenging the industrialised model of education. He imagined a world in which we would encourage children to be free to use their instincts and we would reward them for their difference, flair, and creativity. The independent actor must be free of the chains of conformity and social conditioning, truly able to think independently. Embracing a spirit of rebellion in your work is useful; it will help you stay attuned to your impulses. Your imagination is a never-ending resource, overflowing with ideas and far exceeds the limits that we place upon it.

We may fear we do not have an idea when in fact we have many – our fear of selecting what we perceive as the *wrong* idea prevents us from seeing the wealth of ideas available to us. Fear is the enemy of imagination, and it can make you question whether you have any ideas of worth; it judges you and places a block on your imagination (see Wellbeing). Prioritising your imagination over your logical mind can enable you to avoid fear and to think beyond the mundane. Logic is essential for the actor at the right moment, for example, in research or the analysis of text (see Context and Text). However, if you try to engage logic during imaginative processes it will ridicule your impulses and prevent you from experimenting. Logic will never allow abstraction or expressionism and it will suppress the exploration of a magical reality. Give yourself unlimited permission to unlock your imagination; take the risk.

Journal the results of your imaginative flow so you can reflect on any themes or consciously explore any content that scares you. Use your imagination as both a starting point for your work and a central part of the work itself. Imagination breeds – one bright idea inspires another (see Creativity). Surround yourself with fellow artists who choose to expose their imagination and prioritise it over fear – it will liberate your curiosity and your delight and enable you to become free. This freedom also helps when you are working with practitioners who may experiment with diametrically opposed ideas to those you know.

Only when the audience can witness actors immersed in imaginary circumstances does it inspire them to access their own imaginations and join you. Your imagination brings action and text to life by believing in an invented reality, which is as important as being able to create it. The imaginary circumstances must be clear for the actor to live within them and believe. When the actor is immersing truthfully in a set of circumstances, they cannot help but make connections to personal memories. However, your own personal memories invading the imaginary circumstances can work against the text. It is important to create character-specific memories through improvisation that allow you to draw safely on these memories rather than your own. Character memory is powerful – it exists when your imagination connects with specific moments in the story and makes them live (see Character). It is distinct from 'emotional memory', which demands you play out your own experiences and emotional reactions.

In the exercising of your imagination, it is important to ensure you are looking after your mental health. Your active imagination can resurface any experiences lying dormant in your subconscious – this is not in your control. If you want to be free and open in the moment, you need to be emotionally ready. If you have some unresolved trauma, you may find work on the imagination is too scary until you have engaged with some form of therapeutic help.

Certainly, imagination work requires you to be open and honest with yourself and can reveal deeply buried thoughts or experiences, so make sure you have support in place to enable your goals (see Wellbeing).

Play

Play is the most satisfying vehicle for the imagination and is extremely important for your health and wellbeing (see Wellbeing). The desire to play is natural; children know how to play – they just get on and do it without help or instruction. They instinctively know the 'game' to play and the part they will take; they use their imaginations to invent the activity, to create characters and to picture the setting. You never see a child overthinking *play*, just immersed in it. Play is always active and is about the enjoyment of the act of playing rather than the result of having played. A recreation activity, play is unimportant but fun and designed purely to produce pleasure. Engaging in play as an actor has a seriousness of intent and yet is equally joyful as you are directly seeking to access your creativity, to experience it, to recreate and reflect the human experience. Recreation is the opportunity to replay what we know and develop beyond it, to add our imagination and to create something new.

The opportunities to invent scenarios and create narratives are greater in a group as you have the benefit of collective imagination. The joy of play is more abundant because of this collective imagination. However, if you are taking a self-led approach to acting, there are many ingredients you can engage with alone and your imagination is your limit (see Creativity).

Mischief

- Invent a practical joke you could play on someone close to you.
- Be kind and ensure the recipient can take it in good humour!
- Reflect on the feelings you experience as you invent the mischief and those you encounter as the joke plays out.
- Write these into your journal and refer to them when you are working on a role to inspire ideas for mischief.

Surprise

This is a vital element in drama because it is a constant in life; nothing ever plays out exactly as we imagine it will. Surprise differs from mischief in its intention: it is more normal to delight someone and so the feeling experienced in the preparation is less 'naughty'.

- Create a surprise for someone you know.
- Reflect on the feelings you experience as you create the surprise and those you encounter as the surprise happens.
- Write these into your journal and refer to them when you are working on a role.

Re(-)creation

Find an old photo of yourself, remember the scenario you were in, who you were with and what happened that day.

- Imagine what an alternative outcome may have been that would have radically changed the memory and/or the photo.
- As a stream of consciousness, speak or write their interior monologue (see Character).

Thrill

Explore some activities you may find thrilling – funfair rides, trail biking, skydiving, water slides, climbing to the top of a mountain. Anything that for you will generate excitement rather than fear is ideal. It does not have to be an extreme sport, it can be any sort of adventure, swimming in the sea, climbing to a peak, trying a new hairstyle! Write the experience into your journal and reference this when you are engaged in a role (see Creativity).

As a developing actor, the more you can turn your learning into a game, the more you will find your imagination is working. Imagination allows you to feel that everything is possible, it makes you excited to make progress from a positive mindset. Experiment giving only positive responses to other people and reflect on what returns. This comes with a safety warning: for decades, we have encouraged actors to learn to say *yes* or *yes and* .... The ability to accept and to offer is fundamental in making creative choices and collaborating with other actors. There is no correlation between this and the right of the actor to say no.

In situations where you feel unsafe – such as an abuse of power in the room – you are not obligated to say yes; coercion is not a form of play and has no place in the creative space or in life. There is an important distinction here between saying yes and feeling safe or saying yes because of coercion. If you have worked through your own fears (see Wellbeing) you will have a good measure of the difference between when you are lacking the courage to say yes and when you are unsafe. Your consent is everything and, where it is appropriate, developing a positive response in scenarios can open your imagination and bring a world of surprise, joy and creativity. Risks in the studio or rehearsal room must only ever be *artistic* ones.

Spontaneity

Spontaneity is unplanned behaviour and so you cannot be in control of it – it is a surprise both to you and to your fellow actors. This can be scary and re-emphasises the need to feel safe with the people you are working with. The Coronavirus pandemic had a strange impact on opportunities to exercise spontaneity; the online environment is both a wonderful invention and yet also a threat to spontaneity. We briefly lost the opportunity for serendipity or surprise, the planned timing of every class and meeting was essential and we no longer bumped into each other – this lack of surprise dulled our responses. How vital it is to enjoy and celebrate the freedoms we normally have, and for the actor to find every opportunity for surprise. You can only engage spontaneously if you are truly existing in the moment – you cannot rehearse spontaneity.

Improvisation is the very best way to improve your spontaneity. If you adore being in control, you will need to really focus on developing your improvisation skills. Look for local improvisation classes or devising opportunities. Improvisation terrifies some actors, filling them with dread. There are associated expectations of needing to be 'funny' and it can be terrifying, unless 'being funny' comes naturally for you. The good news is that improvisation, unless it is part of a comedy show, is not about comedy and is only as funny as real life itself. The other fear is the need to be clever – you are after all writing a play on the spot with your dialogue. Remember that the work you improvise is not for an audience; improvisation is a great tool, one to sharpen your responses and exercise your imagination. The feeling of great risk is about fear of revealing your vulnerability rather than anything else (see Wellbeing).

Remember that no one is recording this for posterity unless you are in a devising process for which you will have preparation and warning, or unless you are filming and asked to improvise! Begin by letting the pressures of being funny or clever go and enable yourself to respond through impulse. Your impulses fire from your instinct and you usually feel them in the gut or the heart. Cancel the idea that you can be wrong, the point of improvisation is that it is spontaneous, unplanned and uncensored. By not editing your responses you will become quicker, nimbler, a better listener and more able to respond to the circumstances of the character (see Connection).

Sometimes there is preparation in advance of the improvisation process. This may be in the form of research – exploring how real-life events can come to life, how imagined worlds can be created or creating a backstory for character (see Context and Character). It is useful for writers in a workshop phase to explore character and content and it can also prove helpful as part of the screenwriting process. British filmmaker, Mike Leigh, has long excelled by creating spontaneous conditions for his actors, surprising them to deliver truthful improvised authentic responses. Making his actors only aware of their own character's circumstances, text and action, they are alive and vulnerable to the story as it unfolds.

Become comfortable with taking artistic risks by enjoying the opportunities spontaneity gives you. Always remain within the parameters of the agreed work but immerse yourself in the moment so you can be spontaneous. It will allow you to make bold choices; no audience is interested in bland choices, they crave dangerous, fun, gritty and generous choices. The audience wants to forget the actors know what is going to happen. Spontaneity helps the actor hold the audience in suspense and experience surprise, by not signalling what is to come. The belief of an audience to accept that the words or actions are coming from the live stream of consciousness of the character helps us to make the live moment precious for them.

Storytelling

At some point as an actor, a director will give you the note to – *just tell the story*. Usually this suggests you have over-complicated what you are doing, and you need to go back to the root of the actor's job – to tell the story. Every project you will ever engage in has a story at its core and it is the actor's skill to identify it and tell it. Our desire to tell stories is deep within us and is an ancient connection, the joy of recounting our human experience or inventing scenarios to share with others is a daily ritual for us. We share stories for so many different reasons: to educate or to warn others, to bond with them, to cheer them up, to seduce them, to inflate our ego, to offer a gift, to threaten, to entertain, to reassure. The list really is endless because it strikes at the heart of every intention we can have as a human being. The need to share our stories is active and has great purpose.

Traditions of storytelling are global and must date as far back as our arrival on planet earth because they account for our experience of it. Storytelling is the easiest way to win trust, develop friendships, discover love bonds, and reconcile conflict. It enables us to imagine new ways to live and to see ourselves reflected. The oral tradition of storytelling is a wonderfully creative form, shapeshifting as it passes on through communities and across generations. Fables, folktales, proverbs, epic histories, myths and legends are told to create legacy, teach heritage or incite change. The telling is often intimate, creating a sense of ceremony or ritual.

Storytelling traditions across each continent have their own cultural expertise and flair, both within the stories and their delivery – whether with dance, song, call and response, imitation of stock characters, puppetry, movement, mime, light, music, costume and make-up or the atmosphere of a sharing circle. The story may be re-enacted spontaneously by a village elder or given a fully rehearsed enactment involving the community. Storytelling happens anywhere, in a pub or a sacred space, a fireside or community hall, a theatre space or a market and it is often at its most magnificent outdoors in nature.

Traditions of storytelling are specific to the needs of each community. Playing the important role of oral historian or keeper of ancient wisdom, the storyteller has been a universally respected figure. The Native American storytellers passing on stories of the land, spirit and origin of the tribes, East African stories telling of trickster animals, the West African Griot using song and music to communicate story or the Irish Seanchaí moving from town to town, regaling ancient lore. Traditions have evolved, merged and been shared over time, enabling a rich melting pot of forms to inspire next generations. Western theatre has without doubt benefitted from these storytelling traditions and cultural appropriation has largely been unacknowledged. Over the centuries, native storytelling traditions were impacted by imposed colonialist cultures and cultural preservation has been difficult to maintain worldwide (see Text).

Passing on stories is the great skill of the actor; it requires your imagination to influence the imagination of others. Working unscripted you can develop spontaneity through the art of storytelling. Engage with your own stories, the current stories you need to tell, the stories in your family within your lifetime and those from your ancestors. In communicating these stories, you perform a role as the keeper of your history. It is a wonderful way to connect to your own identity and a great way to practise sharing your authentic self with others. When we hear stories, we are inspired, or distanced by the characters in the scenario; we imagine ourselves as characters in the story, we assess the actions of the characters and we engage empathy and understanding to make sense of it all. The listener, your audience, will want to develop a deeper connection with you as you tell your story and as they recognise and imagine themselves within it. Imagination is the greatest gift of the actor.

IMAGINATION

- Trust instinct, follow your curiosity and delight.
- Instances of: Mischief, Surprise, Recreation and Thrill are catalysts.
- Risks must only ever be artistic ones.
- Say yes, and …
- Tell the story.

CHAPTER SIX

Connection

We strive to be seen, to be heard or to be acknowledged by another human being; we aim to be witnessed, to be accepted and to experience human closeness. Only by connecting with others can we learn empathy. Understanding the human need to find connection to others is at the heart of being an actor. Empathy is an essential element of your work and connection is the key. Connection between actors and connection in the scene and the world of the play are essential.

The first part of this journey is to connect with yourself. Who are you? What is your gender identity, ethnicity, heritage, age, socio-economic background, sexual orientation? What are your experiences in the world, your geographical location, your values, your lifestyle, your political beliefs, your family connections, your interests? Some of the above may change during your life through choice and experience and others will not because they are your birth right and factually accurate.

- Consider how each of these elements of your identity shapes how you feel and how you see others?

- How do these affect how you respond to situations?

- How does your identity help to form your experience of the world?

- How do you present your authentic, genuine self?

This self-interrogation will help you to sit more comfortably in your own skin and to understand your own ideas and behaviours. Be kind to yourself and work to accept all that you are (see Wellbeing).

You are unique and your identity shapes your actions. Part of embracing life as an independent actor is very clearly understanding yourself and becoming your strongest advocate. The actor who owns their identity and embodies all that they are is powerful.

Draw a map of the self …

- Draw an outline picture of yourself in the centre of a large piece of paper.
- Write the information most precious to you inside the figure such as your identity.
- Surround it with other information that distinctively identifies your tastes and choices.
- Reflect on the whole picture.

Connection is possible only when *you* are truly present – freely existing in mind and body to the moment you are in. Being present means momentarily relinquishing the past and avoiding the anxiety or intrigue of the future. Being here, now. So simple in concept but hard to accomplish, it takes a good deal of practice to achieve this state of being. It is enormously liberating when you do achieve it but sustaining it is the real challenge. To become truly present you must choose to accept the past as fact and the future as fiction. No degree of reflection will change the past – the moment you are in is the result of the past and therefore immovable. Planning and dreaming can change the future but no degree of planning or dreaming can make the future a fact in this moment. Knowing where we are right now and what we desire – this is the space in which the actor must exist.

Your character's wants can only be played in the present and the dramatic conflict experienced by the audience results from watching your character in the moment as their story unfolds. The difficulty often experienced by actors in long rehearsal periods or long runs is that the body has had time to process the journey of the character and so the events that unfurl in the moment are no longer surprising to them. Believing solely in the knowledge and experience your character has in the moment is vital, particularly if you are performing eight shows a week for six months or longer. Equally important is 'unknowing' the rest of the plot and how it plays out. Your character must have expectations in the moment which are based on *now* and not on anticipating the action in future scenes or knowledge of how other characters will respond.

Listening

Listening is an element of the actor's work that requires ongoing practice. Starting from a place of *being* rather than *doing* is useful. Listen to those around you in your day to day and truly commit to hearing what they say. This means you are doing the opposite of waiting to speak and you are not making assumptions on what you hear, based on your expectations of what you thought they were going to say. Your communication will improve immeasurably by doing this. Staying in the present moment and committing to listening will stop you anticipating. In the first instance you are simply trying to remove the urgency to have your turn.

When we listen, we are searching for the connection between what the other person is saying and ourselves. We want a part of their speech to connect to us, our experience, our beliefs, even direct references to us. We want to recognise a hook we can latch on to and which in turn triggers us to respond. It is rare in conversation for a person to allow another to finish speaking, to take time to consider what they have said and then to respond. Often, we have the compulsion to speak mid-sentence and rather than just listening, we wait patiently for speaking to end, so we ourselves can speak.

Listening, for the actor, must strike a balance between real life behaviour and the construct of reality – albeit a rehearsed one. Truly listening to your fellow actor helps you find the trigger that compels you to speak your line. However, for them to finish their dialogue you must find a way to suspend the moment and retain your impulse to respond. Really good writing enables the actor to suspend their impulse to speak because the line they are hearing remains pertinent to them. In real life we do not know how long someone will speak for, it could be five seconds or four minutes and is driven entirely by their need to land their point. Once we feel we have landed our argument, or provoked a response, or got something off our chest, or confessed a secret, we stop speaking – so too for your character.

Creating the conditions for connection involves ensuring you are present, open and energised. Then you must commit to the art of listening, which lies in relinquishing control, allowing the moment to lead. It will help you if you make the moment all about the other person. Placing your focus on them helps to keep you in the moment. Listening helps to inform reaction, which is crucial to the storytelling, particularly on screen. Truthful interaction can only happen when the words you hear have impact, if you truly hear the words a character speaks, they will motivate your response. Reaction then becomes the catalyst for action.

Eye contact is very useful as a starting point for connection; you see into the truth of the actor in front of you and by maintaining eye contact you agree to share a vulnerability. Of course, in real-time conversation, it is very unusual to maintain full eye contact continuously with someone, unless you are about to kiss and become intimate.

Energy

Energy is the life source for connection, and ensuring that you have high energy will enable flow in your connection to others. When you sit, it is harder to retain energy, so if you are in a scene where you are required to sit for any length of time, try using your sit bones at the base of your pelvis to help you remain connected. Developing your energetic levels can be done by ensuring you exercise regularly to help the oxygen flow through the body. In addition to this you can become attuned more keenly to your energy source by placing focus on the chakras through warm-up or meditation (see Wellbeing).

Our chakras are subtle energy points that enable the flow of energy through our physical body. They are often described as wheels or energy centres, and they are positioned from the top of the head following the direction of the spine through to its base. There are many ways in which we may connect on a deeper level with our chakras: yoga, reiki, massage, meditation – each of these offers a connection that can help you to experience energetic sensations in a more profound way (see Wellbeing). Once you have experienced these sources of energy it is easier to reconnect with them when you need to.

The seven chakras run vertically from the top of your head all the way down through the torso. Each chakra is related to nerve cells and organs and the positions are known as: Crown, Third eye, Throat, Heart, Solar plexus, Sacral, Root. The thought of connecting with your chakras may feel like a rather airy concept. Challenge yourself to put aside any preconceived notions and try it. See a reiki practitioner to be introduced further to your chakra energy points or engage in spiritual-led yoga or meditation.

Connection not only demands energy, it also requires a level of vulnerability, a willingness to reveal yourself. If you are confident and really know yourself, this will be much easier – exposing your vulnerability is your choice and it should always be done safely. If you are ever required by a director to go further than you feel safe to, just say no (see Wellbeing and Space). You have the right to keep yourself safe and only you know what is 'safe' for you, so you can positively commit your vulnerability.

Emotional connection to the action and/or the text is what brings an audience the illusion of truth. This is not to underestimate the level of truth an actor must commit to but ultimately, the audience receives a constructed truth. This can be very helpful for the actor who invests a high level of emotional vulnerability to connect within a role. At the end of a performance or rehearsal, find a moment to stop and remember that what has happened in the room is make believe, reassure your emotional self that you are safe and enable yourself to switch back into your life (see Wellbeing).

Emotion memory is not a useful technique in the theatre in my experience. Actors can draw on personal memory to evoke a heightened emotional response, but this is flawed. Whatever the memory is, it will never exactly match the conditions your character is experiencing. Their given circumstances and personal history are different to yours and so your response may be inaccurate. The result of drawing repeatedly on real emotional trauma will either reduce its weight over time as you heal, or make it retreat and impact your future mental health.

Imagination is our greatest tool and when it connects with your emotional resource you can produce extraordinary results. Your experience of the world, of love, pain, joy, of observing others in high stakes situations, is essential for your acting. It gives you an ever-developing library of understanding and feeling, which can be accessed by your imagination. Uta Hagen and Stanislavski, amongst others, advocated directly accessing personal emotional truth, only later to reject this in favour of a focus on the character action as the driver for emotional truth. You cannot unlearn your emotional experiences and they will always inform your acting and, if your focus is on imagining the stakes for the character rather than yourself, you will arrive at a safer and more relevant outcome. The imagination will naturally access the elements of your experience it needs to satisfy the demands of the role, without you deliberately drawing on them (see Imagination).

Endowment

To find connection to action or to another actor, you need to establish familiarity. Rather than seeing the actor opposite you, it is important to see the traits of their character and to endow them with the action their character takes. On this basis your character can make the relationship active – endowment allows context to become playable. If the character is rumoured to have abandoned their child, for example, your character needs to see this when they see them. It allows you to impose character opinions and allows your imagination to lead. Interaction is not simply about the immediate circumstances, words and action. Every moment has historical context (see Context), which informs the circumstances, words and action. This may be simple – two people who are meeting for the first time bring no knowledge of each other, but they do bring their own history, flaws, desires, assumptions and expectations. Or they may have information about the other, which influences their communication.

We cannot help but bring ourselves to every interaction we have in life despite often doing our best to hide elements of this. The truth of your character interactions will rely on what you see when looking at the other character. Making the moment about the other person means you see them for what you feel they are and communicate with them on this basis. Believing is the key to endowment – you must believe in what you endow on another actor. Endowment is always intrinsically linked to the given circumstances and so you need to be imaginatively invested in the scenario.

Endowment can help to create more specificity in your acting and much of the object work you may encounter touches on this. We spend our lives surrounded by objects, which may have a practical use, give us aesthetic pleasure or link us to memories. A toaster, a sculpture, a photograph. And yet these objects rarely exist on a single plane. The toaster may be broken, the sculpture may have been a romantic gift, the photo may be fading. Each object represents more than its physical form. It connects us to a part of our life. Why am I holding on to a broken toaster? Can I afford to fix it? Does it represent a moment in time when I bought it? Does the sculpture work in its surroundings or am I displaying it because it represents the person who gifted it? Does the fading photograph represent my memories receding? Simply by endowing each of these objects with the simplest context, you create layers of character memory and there are questions that emerge and could open a variety of avenues.

We often search for meaning in objects and take physical comfort in the attachments they represent. Finding the objects for your character (see Character) is an important element of preparation. Objects may feature in the script and be seen by an audience, equally they may only bear a significance to you and act as a hook into feelings and thoughts. They can be as simple as a stone, as complex as a diary or as expensive as a diamond. Identifying what the objects are and what their significance is in the character's life is the important thing. Once you have sourced or been given the object, it is for you to endow its significance and meaning. Your relationship to it and who or what it may represent will only flourish if you commit to your belief entirely.

Endowment is also essential when working on fight scenes. In theatre you work with a fight director and will need to achieve all the action that is choreographed. To an audience it will appear that your character has been punched or kicked but of course it is safely organised to appear that way – endowment is essential to keep the actor safe. For us to believe this, we rely on you endowing the fight as if it were happening for real. Where does the punch land and what does it do to you? Reacting to this will only be possible if you endow the punch with your imagination. In high intensity dramatic film action the actor may well be substituted with a stunt person to ensure safety.

Endowment is regularly used in improvisation exercises. You partner with an actor and you allocate them traits and backstory. This then activates some character ownership for them and allows you to explore your character relationship with them. At the root of all endowment work is the fun of bringing your imagination to intersect with the given circumstances. In work that relies on a heightened style of physical storytelling we often use a chair to become a car, a ladder, a dancing partner. The power of endowment is seen clearly in these instances – when you believe it, we believe it (see Imagination).

CONNECTION

- Know and reveal yourself.
- Develop empathy.
- Commit to eye contact, listen, and hear.
- Emotional availability.
- Connection with people, places and things – believe.

CHAPTER SEVEN

Context

Context is everything that surrounds the text you are working on; it sits alongside the text, which is informed implicitly by it. Without context we cannot form a holistic understanding of the text or its themes or make acting choices that are fully relevant. You can only begin to fully understand the context of the script and the research required by reading it multiple times.

> Read the text each time for a new reason, to separate the layers of discovery and enable your deeper understanding:
>
> 1 for comprehension
>
> 2 for context and to identify research
>
> 3 for character and circumstances
>
> 4 to understand structure to analyse content
>
> 5 to make sense of your research
>
> 6 to learn and assimilate.

World of the play

To engage your imagination and immerse in the action, you must fully comprehend the world of the play; this applies to theatre, screen or audio scripts. It may accurately represent the world as you know it today, be set in an historical moment, be an imaginary world created purely for the purposes of the work, based on fact, or thriving on fiction. Understanding this will help you to understand the function of your character within it (see Character) and give you clues to the style of performance.

Exploring the world of the script gives you a creative opportunity to imagine a world beyond your experience – a world you might otherwise never know. It requires you to engage in research to immerse fully in the underpinning facts of the world – even when the landscape is entirely invented, there will be references to draw on from other attempts at fantasy. For example, the non-existent society of Utopia, coined in 1516 by Sir Thomas More, derived from the Greek word for 'no place' and presented a world with an almost impossibly perfect community and political system. To embark on an imaginative understanding of such a perfect world, you must gain an understanding of what is broken in our current society to then make the imaginative leap to its opposite.

Dystopian settings (the opposite to perfection) are even more likely to be the starting point for the dramatic world as they are so rich in potential conflict. By creating a fantasy world, the writer can easily take licence to populate it with unknown fantasy creatures or sci-fi inspired characters. The power of your imagination is extraordinary, and it is essential to work on making it expansive and flexible. However, to invent, the writer usually starts with a world they know before inverting, embellishing or deconstructing it. For the actor too, your anchor must be the world you know so you have a base truth to work from. You can imagine and invent beyond your experience using this real-world anchor to help you create opposites. The more you live fully in the world the greater your imaginative power to move beyond it and break its rules.

Answering the fundamental questions will give you a starting point to understanding the world of the script:

1 Why has this been written, what themes are explored?
2 Where is it set, what is the specific location?
3 When is it set, what period, what is the time frame?
4 Who are the characters and what are their relationships?

5 What happens, what scenarios and events play out to create the drama?

6 How is it constructed, what style, what conventions are used?

Only by answering these questions can you immerse yourself in an understanding of the script beyond just a surface read. Record your answers fully and be accurate as you use this information to source further clues.

Research

For many actors the notion of research can feel counterintuitive, an *academic* approach to acting rather than a practical tool. The key to dispelling this fear is to understand that research is practice – the academic-related word *praxis* describes practice and theory as the same, united through action. In short, research is active, and the job of the actor is to include it in their practice. Research must be detailed to bring your work depth and specificity. It is one of the opportunities during your creative process to fully engage your curiosity. When we are curious, we have a front-footed drive to discover answers. If you are truly curious this will never be a chore – research brings knowledge and knowledge is power.

In your reading of the play to uncover context you will have mapped out in your notes what you can derive from your reading of the script. Now you are looking to identify what you *do not know*. Research is started by identifying a list of questions you want answered. Start by making a list based on the findings you have, which will dictate possible areas of research. If you are researching well, you will generate too many questions. The skill you will develop is when to limit the questions you choose to answer or how much depth you require to fulfil your needs. Selecting appropriate and useful research that you can actively incorporate is your goal and this mainly requires common sense.

It is extremely useful to be methodical when you are researching. Every question you ask will usually populate a range of different sources to explore. Record the answers as you discover them and keep a record of where you found them – this helps you retrace your moves if you need to or enables you to share the source with other actors. This can include noting down timings of a particular scene in a film or audio resource or using tags in books to help you relocate items. You may wish to photograph elements of your research if you find answers visiting a location or if you are looking at various artefacts. Keeping these in a journal also retains them for the future if you revisit a role or you are researching similar themes, time periods or activity.

Let us imagine for example that the script is an epic love story set during the Italian campaign in the latter part of World War II. Taking each of the fundamental questions, you may discover the following answers, which could in turn promote some of the following questions:

1 *Why has this been written, what themes are explored?*

Answer: Political moment of war or conflict exploring a theme of the triumph of love and peace over violence and hate. It promotes the idea of hope as our greatest weapon.

Possible research questions: What are the specifics of the conflict, what was the Italian Campaign? How did it begin, what was the political situation? How did it end? Who were the casualties and how did it change the course of the war? What examples of love and peace intervening are there? What were the strands of hope during the conflict?

2 *Where is it set, what is the specific location?*

Answer: Monte Cassino, Cassino, Nr Rome, Italy

Possible research questions: What is the significance of Monte Cassino to the story? What role did Italy have in the conflict? Why is it set in this location rather than say Calabria or Sicily? What is the historical, social, political and economic significance of this location? What is the cultural landscape of the region? What is the climate like during the period?

3 *When is it set, what period, what is the time frame?*

Answer: January–May 1944

Possible research questions: What is the social and historical background? What specifically happened at this time in Monte Cassino? What were the living conditions during war in this period for allies, Germans and Italians? How does the time frame inform the action?

4 *Who are the characters and what are their relationships?*

Answer: Fifteen characters, Italian, English, Polish, American and German. The female protagonist, Lucia, is a daughter of Mussolini who falls in love with the male protagonist Freddie, an English soldier. Some characters meet other characters but no one scene incorporates all characters.

Possible research questions: What relationship did each of these nationalities have to the Italian campaign? Who was Mussolini? Did Mussolini have a daughter named Lucia? Which characters are aligned to which element of the conflict? What was life as a soldier like during this conflict?

5 *What happens, what scenarios and events play out to create the drama?*

Answer: Fighting, romance, disguise, betrayal.

Possible research questions: What real life examples of such scenarios from the campaign are available? How was the battle of Monte Cassino fought? What examples can I find of romance between enemies? How was disguise utilised in operations during World War II? Were there rewards offered for betraying your comrades?

6 *How is it constructed, what style, what conventions are used?*

Answer: The action moves fluidly back and forth between the five-month period of the script through flashback. Some characters narrate sections of the action and then become a part of it. Acting style is realistic but the form is stylised.

Possible research questions: Are the conventions used typical of this writer's work? What films for reference play out of chronological sequence? What can be discovered if I assemble the script in the chronological timeline?

Sometimes by answering the first question you ask you will discover a raft of other better-related questions, and this enables you to put some of your initial questions to one side. Often the same question will be generated more than once, which suggests its importance. The process is intuitive and when you feel lost go back to the script and remind yourself of why you are choosing these questions to research. The list of sources for your research will be generated by the questions you want to answer. Essentially, anything that leads your path to finding answers is research, and there is no prescribed route to getting there. Remember too that your primary source – the script – will hold key information. Once you know the questions you wish to start with, you can look for 'leads' – information that helps you explore any number of other sources.

Action	Where	What
Reading	libraries, internet	books, diaries, press articles, scripts, blogs, social media
Watching	theatres, cinemas, television, internet	film, TV, documentaries, plays, vlogs
Viewing artefacts	museums, galleries, outdoor locations	exhibitions, installations, collections, photographs, buildings, ruins
Listening	smartphone, radio, in-person interviews	podcasts, speaking to people who have specific lived experience or an oral history of the topic

Once you have accessed some sources to answer your questions and documented a record of what you have found, your next challenge is to apply what you have learnt. In our invented scenario, more understanding of the conditions of war and the level of stakes evident for your character will likely be your first considerations. How do these impact your physical, vocal, behavioural choices? Knowledge gained from diaries or documentary evidence will often inform your text choices and visual and audio references, or location visits will empower your imagination (see Character).

Sometimes an element of research does not make sense until you have spoken with the director or writer or until you are in rehearsals. Specific research into character competencies can be a lot of fun. For example, your character may make their own clothes, be outstanding at card games or speak another language.

Practising these is also research and vital to finding authenticity in your choices (see Character and Creativity). Research can inform improvisation work in rehearsals, drawing on knowledge from the world of the play to inspire scenarios for playing.

Research can also take the form of finding out more about the creative team or production company you are working with, the venues you may be playing, the filmmaker or the writer. Whatever it is that you are committed to discovering, remember that maximum efficiency with minimum effort is your goal. Research may also include a wider knowledge of the artform – for example, a study of theatre history to place genre and style in context.

The sooner you have answers to your questions the sooner you can engage your findings creatively. Remember too that we all bring our own implicit bias to everything we do, so be mindful of this when you are identifying your questions so that you do not narrow your search unintentionally.

CONTEXT

- Multiple reads will open layers
- Explore worlds beyond your experience
- Find clues, ask questions, uncover more questions
- Do not let your bias narrow your search.

CHAPTER EIGHT

Text

A script is a starting point, it is not intended as standalone literature even if it is written as a play. The production is everything – we see unconvincing texts that are beautifully produced and astounding texts that are poorly produced. Scripts are written with the sole purpose of bringing them to life on stage, on screen or through audio media. To transition from the written form to physical and vocal realisation there will be adaptions made by the writer and director or others in the creative team, yet it is only the actor who can take the text off the page and make it live. So, any script should be seen as a work in progress of which you are fundamental, rather than a finished work of art to which you must aspire.

What defines a good script? Whilst you can examine structure, plot, character, style, language, theme and purpose to reach a definition, there is no true answer to this question which could unite everyone, because taste is personal. Theatres play a key part both in the development of new scripts and more generally by raising the profile of writers through their selection. Texts are chosen for very different reasons and are naturally biased towards the purpose they have been selected for. For example, the Royal Court Theatre in London is an incredible hothouse for championing new writing with a heritage unparalleled in the UK. However, the new writing they are looking for at any given moment in time will consider the socio-political climate, will need to work with their current artistic policy, their financial position – cast size and design requirements, to seek plays that will balance their programme, consider whether the writer is known, what the box office risk is, what are the cultural trends, what is in the zeitgeist? Every choice is deliberate and every theatre is curating these choices.

Inevitably, for every new play that is championed there will be many plays discarded and some of these will remain hidden gems. A theatre without a new writing remit will struggle to put new writers in the mix at all as they are not set up to take the risk – their audience does not expect it. Scripts that have been championed over time by the gatekeepers of new work – literary managers, agents, artistic directors, programmers – will be more readily in circulation for actors to source. When you are looking for plays to read or work on, try to start with texts that may connect with who you are. For example, my preference is always for plays that feature female protagonists and I tend to explore those that experiment with magical realism – I am a feminist and a dreamer. Find text that speaks to you. In doing this you will gain confidence and you can then widen your frame of reference.

Prior to large-scale colonisation in the seventeenth century by Europe – predominantly driven by the United Kingdom – performance was created in every part of the globe, unique to its population and an authentic expression of its people. We know that performance traditions are traceable on nearly every continent and have been particular to every country in the world. This rich difference was diluted at points of colonisation when colonising forces imposed their ideas and behaviours on indigenous peoples. Colonisation during the Renaissance was led by wealthy monarchies in the pursuit of power and this period is almost entirely and wrongly associated as a time of European artistic growth. This 'growth' was in fact the result of plundering other cultures to suppress their artistic ideas and to substitute them with Western culture. The Enlightenment period, known as the Age of Reason, in its rethinking around human authority, human rights and responsibilities clearly should have relinquished the powers of Empire – but it did not.

So, the high art hierarchy, once wilfully constructed by the colonising forces, has skewed the narrative and confused our understanding of rich artistic cultures elsewhere. This has placed the written word at the top of the performance hierarchy, and it has been considered important above all else. A collection of Eurocentric white male writers has been celebrated as the global pinnacles of achievement: Shakespeare, Voltaire, Goethe, Coward,

Ibsen, Chekhov, Shaw – the list is endless. Whilst the Western tradition has been stuck on them as exemplars of great writing, it has ignored writing and theatrical traditions from most of Africa, Asia, South America, the Middle East and essentially much of the world. Whilst it is fair to say that these white male Western writers are fascinating to study and highly skilled in their craft, we should consider them as the tip of the iceberg and not the iceberg itself.

Women have also largely been ignored or lost across the centuries and never promoted as writers, as this would have afforded them power. Indeed, look to any marginalised or historically excluded group and you will find a lack of investment in their writing or a lack of prioritising of their voices. Within this you will also find intersectionality between groups, which further reduces chances. Consider taking up this mantle as part of your own creative growth and start writing alongside your acting career. The more that content is created by and for other voices, the louder it will be heard and the greater visibility it will bring. Writing your own material can be enormously empowering and can present opportunities for you to produce your own work.

Structure and style

The 'well-made play' was coined in the nineteenth century by French dramatist Eugène Scribe and has evolved little since that time. It is depicted by a tightly knit plot and convincing narrative, but it only takes us so far in understanding the basics of play construction as it follows a predetermined pattern and often does not explore characterisation, theme or intellectual ideas.

Its dramatic elements comprise the following:

- *Plot* which has secrets known to the audience but are withheld from certain characters. When the secret is revealed, we reach the climax, the protagonist then has their dignity restored.
- *Exposition* is paid careful attention to during the first act. In later acts the action becomes more contrived to create

suspense – discovering surprise through action or devices such as opening a letter.

- *Reversals* take place in the form of the protagonist having a run of failures and successes with the antagonist.
- *Discovery* involves the antagonist learning facts that they could use against the protagonist in some way. This is not usually known by the protagonist immediately.
- *Misunderstanding* takes place and is known to the audience but not to the characters. This increases the suspense.
- *Denouement* (culmination) is believable, drawing together all strands and resolving or explaining them.

Plays that include these elements follow a five- or at least three-act structure. In recent traditions theatre has reduced to a two-act structure and in many instances now even favours a one-act structure without scene divisions. Audiences have less time and less interest in retaining concentration for lengthy plays. Our viewing patterns tend to be based on film or TV lengths and viewing anything for longer than 100 minutes is a challenge. Exceptions break this rule, of course, but it is fair to say that we prefer intense experiences rather than rambling ones these days.

Not all scripts are carved up into acts or scenes but there is usually an indication of the division of contents. The story or 'narrative' is an account of connected events. This may be led by a narrator figure or through the action of the characters themselves. The narrative is based on a premise, which is the proposition offered by the play – essentially the idea of the play is proved as the action unfolds from its constructed elements. The setting is the place, location and its surroundings, which serve as a background to the play. The narrative may be constructed in a linear or non-linear form:

- Linear narrative – chronological sequence of events that form the story. The most common form, allowing the audience to experience events chronologically.

- Non-linear narrative – deliberate choice to impose abstract sequences or disrupt chronology. This creates a puzzle for the audience and a more complex task for the actor.

Non-linear narrative is generally more challenging for audiences and artists and a good model of this is reverse chronology. Good examples of reverse chronology include *Betrayal* by Harold Pinter (1978) and the musical *Merrily We Roll Along* by Stephen Sondheim and George Furth (1981), both of which are very useful for exploring how narrative is revealed and what challenges exist for the actor in telling the story backwards. We usually consider a dramatic trajectory, building in intensity through forward chronology, but in both these examples we trace the demise of love to its success through moving in reverse to uncover its foundations. We therefore more keenly notice the tipping points which become our focus of regret for the characters.

Film manages this style of narrative effortlessly; in *Peppermint Candy*, the 1999 film by South Korean Lee Chang-dong, the plot is divided into seven sections punctuated with a longshot from the top of a train as it leaves a tunnel. The first section implies the suicide of the protoganist as he stands on the tracks in front of an oncoming train. Skilfully the film is then constructed in reverse chronology with the train shot slicing each section as a constant reminder. The year 2004 saw *Memento* by Christopher Nolan make use of both forward and reverse chronology, keeping the audience on its toes. The actor working in a reverse chronology play in the theatre has a different challenge than in film. Films more normally shoot out of sequence and the absence of the live element reduces time pressure on the reversed emotional trajectory for the actor. Nevertheless, this type of structure requires forensic work on the script and action to ensure an authentic journey could be played in either direction. Flashbacks are a convention that is much more frequently used in both film and theatre. They are less disruptive to the reception of the linear narrative as they are always within its context and usually used as a device for character memory. Scripts are constructs – even a true biographical account is shaped by the conventions used by the writer to tell the story.

The constructed narratives of verbatim theatre were popular in the 2000s with roots in political documentary and agitprop theatre of the 1970s. Verbatim uses the words of real people, usually created by collecting testimony from those involved in a life event. The testimony is then edited together to construct the narrative. The challenge for the actor is in playing the real person and replicating both their words and their speech patterns, and sometimes their vocal traits and qualities. Alecky Blythe, who is a pioneer of this method of working, has developed recorded delivery techniques enabling the actor to imitate the speech of the real person in real time via an earpiece. Many plays have been written or rather edited in this way and the creativity often sits in how characters can connect when for the most part they are each speaking in monologue albeit on the same topic. Some examples of these plays include: *My Generation* (edited by Alecky Blythe), *My Name is Rachel Corrie* (edited by Alan Rickman and Katherine Viner), *A State Affair* (edited by Robin Soans), *The Permanent Way* (edited by David Hare). The events discussed in verbatim are in the past and exist as reflection, so it is hard to create the drama in an active present.

The term 'genre' refers to the type of story being told and this is very much decided by the playwright or in association with whoever is commissioning them. The writer also influences the style of production through the conventions they embed in the writing. For example, they may write in sections of direct address to the audience, which breaks the fourth wall (see Training and Space) and interrupts naturalistic style. Style is heavily informed by the director and often bears their signature – see the work of Belgian theatre director Ivo Van Hove, for example, who takes complete ownership of the material and reimagines how an audience experiences it, or Daniel Fish in his 2023 version of *Oklahoma*.

Categories of plays are ever developing – tragedy, comedy, naturalism, social realism, magic realism, verbatim, absurdism, farce, ideas plays, intellectual or political plays, horror, sci-fi, epic play, melodrama – and are added to as new writing or performance styles emerge. Categorising plays is not straightforward and invariably one category will intersect with another between genre and style. A play may be a tragedy, ideas play and yet autobiographical such as *Long Day's Journey into Night* by Eugene O'Neill. The categorisation is not important for its own sake, but it is helpful as a framework for discussion with your director or in conversation at an audition. Understanding the genre and style of the work will more easily enable you to assess the skills you need to bring to it.

Breaking it down

Much has been written on the detail of breaking down text and its analysis. Bella Merlin has made great inroads into decoding Stanislavski's ideas in several of her books and in a way that really helps new actors. Likewise, Mike Alfreds, in his book *Different Every Night*, gives detailed advice for actors in making character lists as part of their analysis (see Character and Context). You will discover for yourself what techniques help you and, like most actors, you may change your mind about your process and what works for you as time goes on (see Process).

Stanislavski used the image of a turkey being divided into different sized parts to illustrate the components in a play. By placing focus on the construction of the play, you can be most specific about your choices. Acts divide into scenes, scenes divide into units and units break down as you identify beats, objectives or intentions, and actions. The language to describe each element changes, depending on which practitioner you may refer to. Break down your script before trying to make any decisions about what is going on for your character. Breaking it down to each line then enables you to break it down to the punctuation. Every word written to be spoken gives you a quest to understand why the character is saying these words now, in this order and to whom.

Most scripts identify the scene by stating: the setting, which characters are speaking when, the punctuation (which brings us rhythm and tempo), the stage directions to indicate action and the end point of the scene. Before you break down each scene or 'deconstruct' it, remember that the writer has deliberately constructed it in this way for a reason. Use this to guide your curiosity. If your instinct is to evade what the writer has written it is usually because they have not taken an easy option; challenge yourself to respect their creative input. Breaking a script down requires you to constantly be asking *why*. As you begin to understand why, you become better equipped to make your own creative choices based on their work.

In the process of breaking down the text, you will analyse it to understand the journey. You need to absorb all information that charts:

- the arc of the play
- the arc of the act
- the arc of each scene
- the arc of the character's thoughts.

Breaking down text is about identifying your character's story through the Ws – who, where, what, why, when, and how (see Context) and the timeline of the play (see Character).

Tip: Do a reading of the play where you only say your lines, using the rest of the text and 'feed lines' to analyse when and why your character is compelled to speak.

- What is most important to them?
- What is it that triggers your character's response?
- By identifying what makes your character respond, you can identify their thoughts and the sequence.

As you approach each scene your character is in, you can divide the action into units. A unit is determined by what the character who runs the scene wants. It is a short section or 'chunk' that holds conversation and/or action and usually finishes when a different character takes the lead, the subject changes or an entrance or exit is made. Once you have identified the units, you can move on to exploring what your character wants and from whom. You have already started to consider what is most important to them, which will help you define their wants. A 'want' is usually referred to as an objective or an intention and explains the reason for your character being in a scene. By dividing the scene into units, it should make it easier to now analyse and define the objectives. Stanislavski talks about the character having a super-objective, which is an all-encompassing want driving their existence. Within a scene you then focus on objectives specific to the event itself and the characters in the scene. In theory all these objectives ultimately work towards serving the super-objective.

If you become stuck in understanding your objective, it can be helpful to identify the objective a fellow actor is playing and play its opposite. Whilst it may not be accurate, it can be the catalyst for deciding a new objective if you are feeling blocked. Whatever you choose as an objective, focus on driving it rather than allowing it to be a passive yearning. This will also allow the stakes within a scene to be at the height the action requires them to be (see Connection and Character). When another character wants something from your character, do not make it easy for them to get it – remember this is drama!

If this way of organising your understanding helps your acting process, use it, if it does not then do not be afraid to disregard it once you have tried it. A little like the range of different language given to describe most acting tools, there are various takes on the most proficient ways into being specific when playing text. Do not be put off, there are no rules, just lots of different ways to work. Every actor is unique – you are searching for the approaches that work for you and the vocabulary that helps you access what you need. Just remember that you will meet directors who work differently from you and you will need to be open to their process.

Declan Donnellan in his book *The Actor and the Target* invites the actor to ensure they create a target to aim their endeavours, actions, words towards. When using text, this approach can help you to channel your focus and your intentions somewhere specific. Marina Caldarone helpfully created the *The Actor's Thesaurus*, which lists transitive verbs known as actions. Actions are designed to help the actor translate their desire to do something to their 'target' into a specific and playable word. An action can also be thought of as a tactic that your character uses to achieve their objective. At its best, this method is a fun and free exploration of making it about the other person and in the process helps you to discover specificity. Avoid it becoming a pseudo-scientific exercise where you start overthinking, ensure that you keep the process playful, using it more on your feet than round the table. If trying to action every line is making you feel blocked, it can help you just to use it on the lines you are really struggling for specificity with.

An obstacle is something that is in the way of your character achieving their objective. You may use an action to overcome an obstacle and achieve your objective. An obstacle may be another character, a deeply held belief, a family issue, a financial need, in fact anything that stands in the way of your character getting what they want. Obstacles are useful because they create struggle and therefore conflict; if your character had no obstacle, they could just get what they wanted there would be no story. When you are analysing the text, always ensure you identify the obstacles – it will help you to crystallise your objectives more clearly.

Using text

Never fear text – if you do not understand it, look it up. Words are powerful. Never hide behind not knowing meaning. Highlight everything that is unfamiliar and then research the meaning and pronunciation. By doing this you save yourself possible embarrassment and show yourself to be reliable. Most importantly you will have uncovered clues to character and to choices you can make. Also, know the meaning of lines spoken *to* your character, otherwise your character would ask them to explain themselves! Keep the script with you whenever possible. You will naturally be filtering ideas and questions all the time and it helps to have it easily to hand to refer to or to annotate.

Your first reading of the play is hugely important as your experience of it will form the base layer of all your ideas and understanding beyond that (see Process). Part of respecting the writer's input is to be accurate with the text, so once you have analysed meaning ensure you learn both the text and its punctuation accurately. In some instances, you will also work with the writer and benefit from them directly in understanding why your text is constructed in the way it is (see Process). Film has different rules around this with the director sometimes asking you to improvise or 'ad lib' around the dialogue in pursuit of authentic speech. However, this is not the case in every situation, and you can be caught out if you assume it will be.

With texts written before the twentieth century, lines tend to be longer and may be packed with clauses in a single sentence. The actor uses thought to navigate each element and understand the reason for the character continuing to speak. Using monologues to help you analyse the reason to speak and to continue speaking can be very helpful. The monologue is useful as a training tool but is now outdated as a tool to gain work. Increasingly auditions require you to work in duologue with text from the project. For screen work you may be sent 'sides' to audition with – the term refers to the pages used in a day's filming. There is no single template for what you may be required to prepare for an audition, but unless it is a movement piece you *will* be required to engage with text, so these skills need to be sharp.

Tip: Get into the habit of reading aloud everything you see to improve your confidence in sight-reading: ingredients, newspaper articles, novels, manual instructions, plays. Even reading aloud the stage directions will help you connect meaning and find clarity.

There are many different forms in which to write text and they tend to fall into two categories: prose and verse. Verse is usually unlikely to feature in film unless it is a filmed version of a Shakespeare play. Verse offers a heightened form in which the language creates a visual expression and a theatrical engagement. There are rules around the structure of verse, which are helpful for speaking it and well worth learning, so you may break them when good reason arises. Whilst verse form is impressive, do not let that impact your confidence in using it; practising the speaking of verse will remove the unfamiliarity of it.

Predominantly, Shakespeare used the iambic pentameter as the measurement for his verse, the rhythm of a heartbeat with the accent on the second beat of each of five pairs and with ten syllables in total. In *A Midsummer Night's Dream* and *Macbeth* he used trochaic tetrameter for his fairies and witches – the stressed beat is the first in each pair and is known as a trochee, the line has eight syllables. Shakespeare's plays were published in the First Folio in 1623, seven years after his death. It is in the First Folio that we have the best guide to punctuation as it is intact from the original without subsequent editorial interference. Shakespeare's history plays are written entirely in verse, whereas *The Merry Wives of Windsor* is written predominantly in prose. He moves between forms within his own work. Much analysis is available around this, but the actor must focus on why their character speaks in one form or the other or occasionally both. What function does it serve? How does it help your character express meaning and intention?

Words are so important; we choose our words, and they have consequences. They are gifts, weapons, comforters, companions, food for thought. The *compulsion* to speak text must come from the drive of the character to express something. Once they are speaking remember that if they continue – say it is a monologue – they need *impulsion* to continue. If they ran out of steam, they would stop talking! The energy driving your text is important and helps to steer the scene and build the inherent drama.

In performance, an audience is meeting your character for the first time and needs to understand you so they can follow your action. To establish this, keep your text clear and use a steady pace. Unless you can find a good reason, avoid stressing personal pronouns: I, you, he, she, we, they, him, her, he, she, us, them. Usually, we stress the words that are the subject – a person, place, idea or thing. But in addition to these nouns, we can also accent verbs – these identify action or a state of being. It is less common to stress adjectives or adverbs. Emphasis is usually given to text through pitch range, volume or stretching the vowel sounds. All rules exist to be broken if you can justify your choice.

Punctuation informs breath and helps to signal or highlight the following:

- Tempo – the speed or pace of the text
- Rhythm – a regular repeated pattern
- Language – words in a structured communication
- Repetition – a word or phrase used multiple times
- Rhetorical device – persuasive technique
- Stresses – the accents for emphasis
- Pause or silence – moments of suspension or a stop.

Subtext

The Eurocentric psychological revolution in theatre writing at the turn of the twentieth century, which exploded when Charles Darwin, Sigmund Freud and Konstantin Stanislavski became understood in relation to each other, caused a long trend of naturalism. Every line of text from the plays born from this time holds psychological significance, with characters often concealing what they think and presenting complex behaviours. It is from this point that we have referred to the existence of subtext. What is the character thinking but not saying? What truth is below the surface of an action?

Your character may smile and wish another character well whilst despising them for news they have just announced. It is extremely useful to analyse text from this period and beyond on the basis that subtext drives the internal emotional connection. Shakespeare, on the contrary, was writing before psychoanalysis was born and as such the characters tend to say what they are thinking or feeling. At the very least they will share their truth with the audience!

To help you stay on track with character intentions when you are preparing your work, it can be helpful to use mantras. A mantra is the repetition of an invented line which frames the thoughts or desires of the character. It can be the character objective or the identified subtext or something more visceral. It can even be the last line in a scene – they think it through the scene and finally have the compulsion to say it out loud at the end.

Tip: A mantra can be used out loud by the actor in preparation.

- Choose a piece of text.
- Select an unspoken thought, an intention, a relevant secret, or a line at the end.
- Place these words in the front of your mind and vocalise them before your first line.
- Speak the text repeating the mantra line as often as you feel compelled to.
- Use this repetition to define character motives and find the emotional drive.
- Return to the text retaining the mantra in your head silently.

Subtext is often the motivating force for a character. It is a layer going on beneath what is spoken; quite literally it sits beneath the text and is a great source for the actor to make playing choices. Well-conceived subtext will require solid study on your part to uncover it but holds a rich source of clues for character choices and helps to create the inner life of your character.

TEXT

- Find text that speaks to your lived experience.
- Widen your frame of reference with contrasting scripts.
- Write your own material.
- Find the arc of the play, act, scene, thought.
- If you do not understand text, look it up – knowledge is power.
- Words have consequences.
- Invent mantras to drive the text.

CHAPTER NINE

Character

What is character? Why is the actor in disguise? How can we make a fictional construct such as character exist? Character has become more of a question than a fixed entity in recent times. The rise of interest and awareness in identity politics and a quest for authenticity has resulted in some interesting shifts in the process of casting, in the parts being written for actors and in approaches to direction. Rather than constructing character based on the writer's invention, actors are finding opportunities to channel their own voice and identity to express character. This makes perfect sense in a time when issues of equity are at the fore and historically excluded voices are beginning to gain opportunity, albeit slowly.

At the end of the twentieth century in *True and False*, David Mamet dismissed the notion of character, arguing that it is created in the writing rather than developed by the actor. A writer of Mamet's standing can easily take this stance but not all writing easily reveals character. Character is the culmination of specific traits or qualities that distinguish us, one from another. In dramatic terms, when creating a range of characters, it helps us to create possibilities for conflict and confrontation, love interests and passion, opposition and harmony. This in turn drives the creation of the plot and the playing out of the story. There are many expertly written plays that examine style, wit, political climate or social justice issues, where the voice of the writer itself is far more fully formed than the distinction of its characters.

Casting is finally becoming more inclusive, with roles opening for a wider range of actors most suitable for their specific casting.

This allows for greater difference to be celebrated in the acting community and this is a great edge forward. The positive results of this change are numerous; for example: the opportunity for a neuro-diverse actor to play the lead role of Christopher in *The Curious Incident of the Dog in the Night Time*, adapted by Simon Stephens; or the understanding that there is no such concept as colour blind casting – we all see colour; or the old assumption that characters are written as white, non-disabled and heterosexual as a default and should therefore not be challenged, which has been exposed as a nonsense.

The challenge is in understanding where *you* are placed and where you *want* to be placed and your agent can help you in defining this. It is complicated, you don't want to be typecast and you do want variety; however, you also want to be able to play the roles for which you were born. Wherever any of this 'lands' for you, once you are cast you will need to consider character. Even if the consideration leads to your decision to play the role entirely as yourself, utilising all your dominant traits, this is a character *choice*. For the purposes of exploring possible routes into character in this chapter we will assume it does exist.

Audiences for theatre, film, television, radio or animation will perceive, connect with, react against, or make assumptions about character based on what is presented to them. It is rarely enough to simply rely on the lines on the page, and you will always be dependent on the medium, genre, writing style and casting, which will determine the work you need to do to bring your fictional construct to life. Whatever your decisions, you cannot *become* someone else, you can only draw on your resources and use them to *channel* character. Your choices at every stage will define the offer of a rounded, believable character.

Traits

Ultimately you are looking for a bond, an empathy with your character – an understanding of why they say and do what is in the script and a search for its justification. This is even more important if you personally consider the character to be morally wrong in their action or thinking or if they hold radically different beliefs to you. As soon as you comment judgementally on your character you are making it impossible to play them truthfully. You must become their *advocate*. Remember it is fiction – whilst you are responsible for bringing the character to life you are not going to be held to account for their behaviour or lack of moral compass. Believe passionately in what drives your character, never comment on the character or compare your views with theirs, it just creates unhelpful judgement. Empathy with the circumstances your character is in and the experiences that have shaped them is essential.

Actors sometimes get stuck with a script or direction and say *'my character just wouldn't say that or do this'*. The reality is that if your character is written to say or do it, or if your director is creating this interpretation, you will need to spend more time getting inside *why* they say or do it. The exception to this is in a devising process or if you are workshopping a new play with the writer present. In these forums the actor is often actively encouraged to contribute feedback on the words and action of their character. On set you may also experience some freedom to paraphrase text in the spirit of wanting you to own the text (see Process). Otherwise, the onus is on you to resolve the contradiction imaginatively and make it work.

Traits are distinguishing qualities of a character and tend to fall into these areas:

- *Personality* – these are the traits that you can fully explore in your character work. It can be helpful to use adjectives to describe how the character is perceived (e.g., closed/jolly/resentful), their outlook (e.g., ambitious/naïve/peaceful) and how they interact with others (friendly/suspicious/overbearing). Some you may instinctively connect to and identify as your own dominant traits and others you may not. It can be creatively rewarding to allow the traits that are less close to you to become more interesting. For example, you may not consider yourself to be a particularly jealous person and yet you have the potential for jealousy in you. If the character behaves with jealousy in the script, explore what the trigger for that jealousy is, so you can understand it and find a hook into playing it believably.

- *Appearance* – this will primarily match *your* appearance – you cannot be shorter than you are for example – but the assistance of wigs, costume, make-up, prosthetics can radically change your appearance. In turn, your changed appearance can inspire your physical choices and help to add specific details in your portrayal of the character that are less common to you.

Your analysis of character will usually start from the script if there is one; this defines the environment and background of the character and importantly the action they take and the words they speak. There have been many iterations of the information an actor can list from their script. Most usefully, Mike Alfreds in his book, *Different Every Night*, suggests various lists for the actor to draw up to capture an analysis of character. To reveal the most exposing information it is important to at least uncover the following:

- What does your character say about themselves?

- What do other characters say about your character?

- What does your character say about other characters?

Write a list for each and ensure you are accurate in copying the words used. These help to uncover what opinions your character has, and the opinions others have on your character. From this information you can begin to construct a truth and centre yourself in the psyche of the character. Spend some time voicing each list of lines and allow this to deepen your grasp on who they are. Consider this with your textual analysis (see Context, Text) to help you gain a fuller understanding of the circumstances of your character.

You have a multiplicity of traits within you, some of which you favour and choose to foreground. Some of these will be in your nature and some are copied through nurture. There will be traits that also lie dormant and unexposed. This gives you a wealth of resources to draw on for your character work. It does not matter how different from you the character may be, you can only use yourself as the channel through which they are manifested. Even when you are playing an historical figure or character based on a true story, the vessel for carrying that truth is you.

Timelines

In rehearsal processes that are geared to psychological realism run by a director such as Katie Mitchell, who has a specifically Eurocentric approach, timelines are everything (see Text). Her book, *The Director's Craft*, gives a detailed explanation of her process, which is heavily influenced by Stanislavski. Whilst it is aimed at directors to help them consolidate their process, it is also an interesting read for the actor. Timelines enable you to make informed decisions around 'before time', which is the period before the play is set, the space between scenes and the period of a scene when your character may not be on stage. Understanding what your character is doing during the play when we do not see them on stage is a vital part of your work (see Character). Katie Mitchell centres her work with actors around these facts to create fully dimensional characters that exist on- and offstage.

If the script or piece you are working on is absurdist, non-realistic, experimental, abstract or in form, then timelines or a psychological approach are less likely to help you. Never dutifully engage in analysis that will not be relevant – it can prove counterproductive.

Where they are appropriate, timelines allow you to consider the concept of time in the script as it plays out for your character. You begin to understand the sequence of events in relation to time and therefore a better understanding of character action and motive.

The timeline is also valuable in comprehending the relationships your character has in the script and to suggest possible backstories to further explore. Knowing your timelines for film is essential. You will need to be clear of the character trajectory in relation to time and place when shooting out of sequence. To play the emotional journey out of sequence in a live setting requires a very disciplined approach to rehearsal in which you will need to plant some continuity to make sense of the reverse structure. In addition to shooting out of sequence, it is common for film to utilise flashbacks, so even if scenes are shot in sequence the timeline may not be linear (see Process). The use of flashback in theatre is less common than film but does exist as a device – for example, in *Forever Yours Marie-Lou* by Michel Tremblay or the David Edgar adaptation of *A Christmas Carol* for the RSC. There are also non-linear examples such as *Constellations* by Nick Payne, which require the actors to have mastery of time (see Text).

Draw your timelines horizontally to really help you capture a visual picture. You may choose to create three timelines or to combine them. Use colours to separate them and help define different elements, which may form useful patterns or reveal interesting hooks.

Timelines		
Timeline of the play	• Where did I come from? • Where am I now? • Where am I going?	Analyse each scene for time span and then piece them together. Scripts that are not structured into scenes will require you to chart the passage of time.
Timeline in between	• Where am I during scenes I am not written in? • What am I doing? • Am I aware of where other characters are?	This may be referred to in the text or you may need to invent this using the facts and your imagination. Have a clear sense of place by creating an anchor to the place your character most wishes to be.
Timeline before the play begins	• What circumstances have impacted my character prior to the beginning of the play?	How far you go back depends on the play. If there are key moments in their life that inform who they are at the start, it is important to include these. Start from birth and assess the character's life holistically if you have the time available.

Timelines are a vital part of your analysis and to build them effectively you must think like a detective. Remember that 'before time' decisions affect your entrances – you always come into the space from somewhere. This detail in the timeline will help you make choices based on how high the stakes are for the character at any point. It can help to chart a visual guide for your emotional trajectory, which for your filming schedule or for rehearsals that are not working chronologically can act as a useful aide-memoire. Once you have drawn the facts together, you can move on to a fun element, which is engaging *imaginatively* with the facts.

Tip: Explore these exercises to help you generate ideas:

- Write the character backstory as reportage.
- Write your character journey as a short story.
- Choose a moment in the timeline and write using stream of consciousness – continuous writing without censorship or edit (see Creativity).
- Read each of these aloud and identify discoveries for your journal.

Hot seating is a popular rehearsal tool with some directors (see Process). I have found it most useful when interrogating characters at specific points in the play to help them uncover what has happened and where they are at emotionally. Using it for *'what did you have for breakfast?'* style questions is limiting and does not really help the actor to build relevant discoveries. More useful is to ask, *'where are you and what has just happened?'* The latter helps them to connect to time, place and situation. Hot seating is a useful exercise when preparing for screen roles; if you have an actor buddy, ask them to help you by asking the questions and commit to remaining 100 per cent in character.

Transformation

Character is manifested by experimenting with your physical, vocal and emotional resources within the choices available to you. If your choices do not contradict the given circumstances, you can play with endless combinations. Some scripts will be prescriptive and specify character physicality and vocal identity. Most usually, the writer has given you the words and the action, but the sound, shape and intensity of playing is all down to you. There is enormous freedom in this element of the work; never wait for the director to dictate character to you, bring prepared options to the rehearsal room so you can originate the choices. A good director will give you feedback and may give you a steer but ultimately character work is your independent contribution. Film and television rarely give you the freedom of a rehearsal period and so the character work must be entirely complete by the time you start shooting. Casting resolves much of this – you are often cast as the nearest actual person to play the role and so you should work on the assumption that they expect the character to be close to you.

Before you start work on your preparation, always find out more about how the director likes to work so you can identify a plan that will best work with them (see Process). Character work can be a solitary activity if there is no director-led exploration. If a physical language is being created in the rehearsal room led by the director, movement director or the company, ensure you make choices that will help you to be a part of the whole. It is disconcerting for an audience to watch actors onstage who appear to be in different plays; bring your character choices into the rehearsal room and allow them to be shaped by the collective effort.

Actors may begin by working from the inside out or the outside in. Remember that ultimately you will need both the inner and the outer to work in unison to have a fully rounded character with an inner life. Some actors work best starting from a physical basis; for example: identifying Laban efforts to put the character on its feet and then explore (see Movement). Other actors work on accent or speech quality (see Voice). There are actors who initially submerge themselves in the psychological facts to find the inner emotional connection and the physical and vocal work comes later. Some actors prefer to learn their lines first and then explore. There is no *right* way of doing things.

You will find your unique route into starting the work and no matter how you start there will be moments when you feel blocked, even momentarily. In these moments try to focus on the physical aspect as this has tremendous unlocking power. Once we lead cerebrally it is hard to quieten the mind. It is also true that you may need to work differently depending on the role, style of the piece, the medium and the director's process, so flexibility is everything (see Process).

In starting character manifestation work with a company, I like to run daily improvisations. This starts with an exploration of the energetic quality of character (see Movement). The actors base this on the understanding of their character from the analysis they have done so far. In identifying the energy quality of the character there is an automatic understanding of rhythm, tempo and breath, allowing the work to have a physical life. The sensations created consume the whole body and generate a momentum to move and exist in the space.

Tip: Try this exercise for yourself

- Choose a character you are working on, stand relaxed in space and close your eyes.
- Allow the facts and your imaginative decisions on character to come into your mind.
- Consider the quality of energy this conjures up – is your character a fast-paced, busy, caffeine-driven go-getter? A lethargic, grumpy, troubled misfit? An optimistic, nervous, inexperienced believer?
- What sensations do you feel when you experiment with placing this energy quality in your gut, your emotional centre? Heighten those sensations as if turning up a dial.
- What image comes to your mind? Look for an active, sensory image, which may be abstract to encapsulate the feeling. Chocolate melting on cold marble and then cracking; feathers in a tumble dryer; bread rising in an oven; butterflies in a bag; wading in a sea of treacle. Allow the image to be abstract, it only needs to make sense to you.
- Use your physical choices for characterisation in the body and consume them with the sensations of this energy quality, associating them with the image you have explored.
- Once your body feels the momentum to move, take yourself into the space and allow the energy quality to express itself through character.

Once actors are moving in the space, they are guided to a sense of place, which may be a location in the script or an invented possibility within the world of the play (see Context). They choose an activity in this place, which may be a regular task, an unusual task or one they have never encountered before. Throughout this they commit to sustaining the energy quality, allowing it to impact the way in which they carry out the activity. Periodically they are moved on to a new location and asked to create more context for being there and for the activity they choose. Props from the play or items that are relevant in the world are distributed in the space for actors to use as they complete their tasks.

We focus on activities they do as part of their work, repetitive tasks that use their body in a specific way and with which they are familiar and adept. This exercise then develops into vocal manifestation with actors speaking lines their characters say about themselves. Repeating the line whilst retaining the energy quality and engaging in activity helps them to explore both the voice quality and the purpose of the line. The voice is therefore birthed from the body and so the work is integrated (see Voice, Movement). The exercise continues until the text is targeted to other actors in the space and eventually being used in first, second and third circle attention (see Connection). This text then becomes the starting point for improvised conversation with other characters. The world is then guided towards characters meeting, conflicts being set up and events unfolding.

Importantly, we never improvise the actual scenes from the play. We will improvise around them or create similar scenarios and play them out and these then have a significant impact on the rehearsal of the scenes in the play. The structure of the writing in the actual scene is easier to maintain if it is not confused with improvised versions. There are opposing views on this of course, including the Active Analysis techniques developed by Stanislavski with his protégée Maria Knebel. Specifically, their *Etudes* directly improvise moments in a scene as an aid to map the play for the actor. Whilst I understand the logic of this work, for me it has never produced results that are as potent as the wider improvisation work. Improvisations to construct character memories outside of the written text are far more useful in my experience.

Our guided long-form improvisation sessions usually last around an hour or so and they can be both joyous and exhausting for the cast. They require complete immersion, no one breaks the imaginative space and by the time we have finished a session it is important to share findings and then have a good rest. It can be quite an emotional process and we must be sure to keep the space safe and nurturing throughout. The discoveries the actors make in these daily improvisations help them create their character language, build a strong experience of relationships with other characters, and the freedom to experiment with choices before they are working a scene. It helps to build the inner life of the character – everything that makes them tick.

This work is unifying, and it is also a great way to break the hierarchy. Every actor takes part regardless of whether they are the lead protagonist or a satellite character with a few lines. It is vital to remember that, regardless of how featured your character is, they are the lead in their own life. The audience have no idea whether your character will have central importance to the story being told or not. This is why it is incredibly useful to fill in the timeline for when your character is not in a scene. These improvisations are also helpful for the company understanding of the hierarchy within the play – it is easier to see the injustices and the power play when you see characters responding to each other live. It reveals the characters who are most isolated and those who are most manipulative.

Tip: Try this extended exercise on your own

- Place a piece of paper with the lines your character says about themselves somewhere easily accessible (if your character says nothing about themselves, you can choose lines they say about others).
- Identify three locations in the space and put some useful props in each area.
- Repeat the energy quality exercise to help you move into your physical characterisation.
- Take your character to a place that is familiar and engage in a familiar task: washing up, digging a flower bed and so on. Explore how they engage physically and what may be distinct from your own habits.
- Find a sequence for the activity which divides into three and explore changing tempos and rhythms within the sequence. Work on repetition until the activity becomes second nature.

- Use the text to hover in your mind almost as a mantra (see Text) and when it builds momentum vocalise the line.
- Repeat the line continuously as you engage in the activity and explore how the line informs the activity and vice versa.
- Move on to new locations and activities and explore the text. Try not to plan your activities, find them in the location in the moment and build character habits.
- Whilst you will not have other actors to receive your lines, you can play with widening circles of attention to help you experience speaking to yourself, to a target or to the world.

Remember to make notes in your journal after a session and record your discoveries.

In real life we change our behaviour and even our voice quality depending on who we are with. These changes happen because of the relationship we have to the other person and what we want from them. Consider in your own life how differently you choose to speak with a close family member or a shopkeeper, a teacher or a therapist, a lover or an employer. Sometimes our behaviour shifts because of the expectations the other person places on us or because we want them to think well of us, we are honouring societal expectations or we are engaging in power dynamics. These dynamics include our historical relationship and how high the stakes are for getting what we want. So too for your character – they are different depending on who they are with and their relationship to them. In fact, the reasons for behaviour are infinite, so never rule any ideas out until you have tried them.

Tip: Explore your approach to addressing different characters:

- Choose a section of your text and speak it to the character cited in the script.
- Choose a character it is not intended for and with whom you have a different relationship and speak it to them.

- Continue to choose different characters, exploring how your communication tactics shift.
- What changes in your pitch, tone, attitude and vulnerability?

If you have an acting buddy (see Training), endow them as each of these characters to help you target the words; if not use your imagination (see Connection).

Identify how being with other characters in the play makes your character feel and behave. Does another character make them feel younger, militant, weary, mischievous, bored? This is about their very presence rather than what they say, necessarily. They will be impacted and affected by others every time they interact with or witness them. Relationship dynamics also change throughout the course of a script, dependent on action. Ensure there is a difference in the way you relate to a character the first time you meet them and later in the script once they have affected you through words or action.

To achieve a full and rounded character, you need to be consumed with every facet of them. Allow your character to behave outside of their normal behaviour by trying out opposites. If your first choice is to explore their natural laziness, then also explore a moment when they may be highly energised. Finding these opportunities for them to act 'out of character' will bring a more truthful portrayal. Look for flaws in your character – they may be big enough to cause your downfall or just be a source of embarrassment, but they will allow your character to be considered human by an audience. Take care not to rely on stereotypes – if you are playing a doctor, for example, it can be far more interesting to explore indecisiveness or low status. Maybe they are a terrible doctor who only scraped through medical school, a socially awkward misfit rather than a high achieving authority figure. You will need to find justification for this, but it will give you a line of enquiry. Refer to *Respect for Acting* by Uta Hagen, whose work on character is a great resource.

Character work is all about finding a way in and creating hooks to lead you on. There are many stimuli that will help in this process. A trip to a portrait gallery can be a great creative stimulus and offer observational detail and inspiration (see Creativity). Music is a powerful tool to unlock the character tempo, imagination, emotional connection and character memory. In long form improvisations I will often underscore these with music from the era, thematic music, or the production soundscape. You can build a playlist to help you access connection or character memories and play it on route to rehearsal, use as part of your warm-up or show preparation, play as your running soundtrack or your meditation soundtrack.

Wearing shoes and clothes that are like your costume can also help with your choices as they impact the way in which you move and behave. If you can access the actual shoes from the wardrobe department, it will help you explore the gait and overall physicality of the character. The difference in feel between a zip or buttons and a high neckline versus a low one is significant. If you are rehearsing a period piece with unusual costume elements such as corsets, bustles or long robes, provision will often be made by the production team to make rehearsal versions available.

Always remember the bigger picture when you attend costume fittings: the costume is not about you, it is part of the *mise en scène* (see Space) and is connected to the artistic choices made by the creative team. The question should always be, '*how can I make my track work in this costume?*' rather than, '*can I have a different costume?*' If there is an issue it will be resolved by the costume team and the director, and they will include you in the conversation when needed. Trust that other people care about their part in the work as much as you do.

Tip: Once you have been fitted with your costume, consider these questions for your character:

- Do they wear these clothes for comfort?
- Do they feel relaxed or uptight in these clothes?
- Did they choose them? Are they handed down?
- Are they practical for the action they engage in?
- Is there an emotional attachment or story linked to them?

These help to reveal imaginative ideas around the choices your character makes and why.

Character work is likely to take up the most space in your journal, helping you through the rehearsal period and on future projects when you are looking for hooks into the work.

CHARACTER

- Authenticity – channelling your voice and identity.
- Never judge your character or their actions, establish empathy.
- Traits – personality that manifests vocally, physically, emotionally; appearance.
- Analysis of text and the three timelines.
- Character preparation best explored through improvisation.
- Your character is the lead in their own life.
- Look for character flaws.
- Use music to unlock character tempo and rhythm.

CHAPTER TEN

Voice

Your voice. It is *your* voice, it can belong to no one else. So unique is your voice that it has an associative emotional impact on friends and family. We recognise voices we know instantly and even Artificial Intelligence (AI) voice recognition software is now apparently able to track the owner of a voice with approximately 95 per cent accuracy. Your voice is unique to you so taking ownership of it is essential. It is the most powerful instrument we own and when partnered with language it has the potential to change the world. Silence is never unintentional, you either choose it or it is forced upon you, it does not happen through chance. Your voice is a large part of your identity and so it is essential to start by understanding and connecting to it (see Connection).

Freedom

In England, speech is historically associated with discipline and accent has been one of the clearest markers of the class system for centuries. In the eighteenth and nineteenth centuries there was an obsession with elocution practice. This is inextricably linked with the imperial spread of the English language in the dominions at the height of the British Empire. The primary purpose of focusing on elocution was to achieve class distinction through formal speech and the wealthy class would show off their privileged education through recitation and practising the art of wit. Across the world, countries have been impacted and influenced by the rulers of empires from predominantly British and European quarters. No less so than through the spread of English as a 'universal language' and with this came the requirement to affect an invented accent – so-called received pronunciation (RP), sometimes referred to as the 'Queen's English'.

Whilst RP is still learnt by actors in the UK, in the best examples of training it is neither an essential requirement nor is it any longer used as the basis for learning other accents – its authority is being dismantled. Undoubtedly there are learning points for the actor in gaining the rigour of elocution, the understanding of rhetorical devices and the flexibility gained by exercising the articulators. However, this approach to the 'art of speaking' which is regimented, absolute and now ancient, unsurprisingly scares off the learner. It sets up a fear of getting it wrong or it imposes false ideas of accent hierarchy, linked to class aspiration. RP became what an actor was supposed to employ as their 'professional voice' and was the primary accent on both stage and screen in the UK.

Vocal freedom, particularly in terms of speech in the UK, is no longer confined to these historical restrictions and other accents are no longer subject to such censorship. With the revitalisation of speech work through panlingual approaches such as the Knight–Thompson Speechwork from the United States, there is an absolute rejection of the outmoded ideas of accent hierarchy. By choosing to place your focus on vocal freedom you can experiment and create authentically. Needing to understand the technicalities can scare off the most curious learner but it will be useful for you to have this foundation of learning. Once you have understood the potential of the sounds you can make, you can focus on how sound is produced and the technicalities surrounding its production. Developing a wide palette of sounds gives you the most creative opportunities. Once you understand the potential of your instrument and you wish to refine its use, the rules become useful.

The freedom to experiment with your voice will enhance your creativity and give you confidence with text. When you are preparing to speak any text, play with rhythm and tempo. Use the punctuation to guide you first then experiment with a range of different rhythms and play around with tempo (see Text). Exploring what may feel like an opposite rhythm and tempo to the obvious helps you to find nuance when you then make your choices. Pitch is another example of how freedom to experiment will bring you creative choices. We tend to think of pitch in terms of singing but we also speak on pitch. We may use our higher or lower register to do so, and we may move freely between these or remain on a single unvaried pitch. To help you find new intonation patterns and pitch range it can be very freeing to sing the text. Not only can this help to release ideas, but it can also help to further reveal the meaning of the text.

The voice follows the body – if you are moving your body in a particular rhythm or in a particular tempo the voice will follow suit. It is quite difficult for them to be in opposition, the voice is part of the body and so they unite. This is both a comfort and a tool to help you achieve vocal goals. If you want more pitch range in the way you are speaking a section of text, you can engage your body to help you. Even raising and lowering your arms will encourage your voice to modulate more. The body is always the answer to unlocking both the mind and the voice. For both the mind and the voice to work in an optimum way your body needs to be released of unnecessary tension (see Movement and Wellbeing). It is easy to forget that every part of the body is inextricably linked and tension anywhere will create tension elsewhere. Using yoga to stretch and then relax the body is a useful approach and equally meditation can help. It can help to play soothing music in the background to help you let go of the tensions you are holding – imagine lying on a warm beach with the sea lapping at the shore (see Wellbeing).

Releasing tension not only gives you freedom but also releases your creativity and energy source (see Creativity and Wellbeing). Tension can be situated anywhere in the body including the face. The release of your forehead when frowning will also help to release tension in your neck. Neck tension can exacerbate jaw tension which is extremely common and results in clenching the jaw closed. To relieve this, gently massage the muscles of your jaw in a circular motion. You can find these muscles under the cheekbones, near to the ears. When your jaw is released, you are more able to send your sound out beyond your teeth. The root of the tongue is also a source of tension and can be alleviated by giving your tongue a good workout by stretching and rolling it in all directions. Freeing the body of its tensions is a valuable part of your whole warm-up (see Process) and it really enables you to do your best work.

Repetition

Your vocal history is intrinsically linked to your body story (see Movement and Wellbeing). There are many elements that have impacted the way in which you speak, how you form your sounds and the way in which you attempt to articulate your ideas and to persuade others.

Training the voice does not mean that you lose the very nuances that make your voice unique. Good training places a focus on learning about anatomy, physiology and breath in order to liberate the voice at its most expressive. It is about exploring the possibilities of your voice rather than changing it. It helps for you to have a grounded learning in these areas to be able to remain consistent and vocally safe, and to deliver optimum results to achieve your goals. At drama school you will work in groups to explore your voice. If you are taking a self-led approach, it can help you to have regular one to one voice sessions with a qualified voice practitioner – this will give you the foundations, experience and a very useful vocabulary.

Most technique in any discipline is learned by repetition, using alignment, knowledge of anatomy, breath and demonstration to replicate a particular exercise which helps you to achieve skill. In voice work you will develop skills by learning how the voice works, use of breath, how to warm the voice up, how to replicate specific sounds, how to achieve clarity and to produce different sound qualities and tone. Just as you would practise if you were playing a violin, your voice is an instrument and to maximise its potential, practise is needed.

Imitation is a fun way to explore sounds that you do not naturally make in your own voice quality or accent. Always ask permission to imitate if you are choosing someone you know so the person understands it as flattery rather than mockery! Watch films and choose actors or people in documentaries to copy. Become aware of what your voice does to change its usual patterns, register, sounds.

Vocal technique utilises exercises which are specific to different areas of your voice work. For example, tongue twisters are specifically used to help increase muscularity and aid articulation. Or, if you wish to explore accents and dialects it is helpful to learn phonetics. By learning this language, you will have the skills to break down any accent into sounds you can then replicate. Explore

The Accent Handbook by Jess Hammett and Lottie Williams-Burrell. Each technical component uses specific exercises and, from there on in, practice is everything. Without practice you will have gained knowledge and some understanding but not application; you achieve the ability to apply your knowledge by accumulation of practice and this in turn enables you to better understand the skill.

Tip: Try these tongue twisters and add your own for regular practice:

- Debbie Dekker dug a ditch, did Debbie Dekker dig the ditchdigger's ditch?
- How can a clam cram in a clean cream can?

Repeat continuously and speed up until you can say them without correction.

Microphone technique is also learnt by repetition which in part explains how the non-trained actor can work in voiceover. Experience in front of a microphone gives you the opportunity to give yourself feedback on what does and does not work. Sounds such as plosives (p k t d g b) are the most difficult to record and whilst techniques such as holding a pencil at a distance from your lips to absorb the sound before it hits the microphone are helpful, nothing beats experience. Practice is experience, you do not need to wait for a voiceover job to practise your microphone technique.

Flexibility

Vocal flexibility will enable vocal transformation, the wider the palette of sounds and qualities you are able to access, the more options will be available for you across the creative industries. There are many ways in which you will be required to use your voice across a range of different media and the flexible actor is always more likely to gain work across the creative industries. Understanding the level of flexibility which will be required of you is important so you can set yourself goals.

For theatre work you may be expected to work in tiny studio spaces seating sixty, right through to mainstage theatres with up to 2,000 seats and every size in between. You may work in different seating configurations such as promenade (see Space) or immersive set-ups with the audience in the same space as the actors. Or you may be in a site-specific piece in a space that is not designed for voice production. Each of these will offer you a different challenge for being heard and understood. The bottom line is that if you cannot be heard or understood, it does not matter how imaginative your choices are, the audience will switch off. Becoming used to playing in different acoustic spaces is important. Listen to your voice in the space (see Process) and notice how live the space sounds. If you are playing in a configuration which means the audience sometimes has your back to them, imagine you are producing sound through your back and ensure you increase resonance and articulation.

Recorded voice for radio drama and audiobooks requires vocal flexibility and a high level of articulation and clarity. The listener is solely reliant on what they hear to be able to construct the world of the play, engage their imagination and follow the plot and characters (see Context and Character). Whilst character authenticity is essential, the preparation work must also include exercises to ensure clarity. If you commit to the punctuation, it will help you to create clear meaning which contributes to our reception of what we hear. Clarity is not exclusive to a particular accent, you can be clear in any accent, you simply need to ensure you use the consonants and vowels that are present in the accent. Avoid feeling pressure to change your sounds toward RP, it is a question of being clear and consistent with the sounds you do make, so an audience can recognise what you are saying. Once an audience has tuned into your accent they will relax and be able to process your spoken text more quickly.

Animation voiceover is closer to radio drama than an audiobook. You are playing the character in scenes with other characters rather than narrating action. If you are playing an animal, use your knowledge of their body conformation to help you make vocal choices. For example, if you are voicing a hippo consider the external rhythms and tempo of a hippo and use those as clues to locating their voice. Think of the elements (see Movement) – if you had the choice between earth, fire, air and water to encapsulate their movement, which would you choose? This also applies to your vocal choices, so if you choose earth what might that sound like? Or you may be voicing a fantasy character such as a unicorn, a child's toy or other usually inanimate object – again use the visual representation of these to inspire the choices you make. Consider what personality the writer has endowed on the character – how does this manifest vocally?

Whilst the finished product of screen animation has the benefit of the visual action, and an audience will not rely on your voice alone, the process of recording is more like radio drama. The actual animation is developed to follow the timing and pattern of the voiceover, so the more dynamic your vocal choices the more exciting the visual representation. Recording for animation voiceover is likely to be in a sound booth in isolation and the visual element of the animation itself will be united with the voice later. Very occasionally it works in reverse with you working to the pre-existing animation, but this is much rarer. Vocal rigour, consistency, range and flexibility are key to this form of work as is the ability to improvise with rhythm and tempo (see Process).

Screen work requires you to use your voice to be heard and understood but usually with the conceit that the character has no awareness of an audience or the live meta event. Often when watching film, we are drawn to our screen to fully hear and understand the dialogue – to retain authenticity some actors refrain from consciously articulating their words. The result can be that it is difficult to decipher what is being spoken, which results in actors being criticised for mumbling. It is an interesting debate, film clearly requires the actor to own the words and action most authentically; life is recreated on screen in a way it can never be in the theatre.

On stage we accept the convention that to be heard and understood the actor must articulate well and send the sound around the auditorium with energy. For screen, you should be working to reach your fellow actor rather than the camera, but it is important to assess the distance of the microphone from you. Whilst screen acting does not require the same use of resonance or volume to project in the way that live theatre does, it nevertheless does require vocal energy. The character is still choosing to speak, which is an active decision. It is important to commit to the text so that this need to speak is authentic.

Vocal health

You use it every day of your life and yet you probably take it entirely for granted! It is important to look after your voice by considering your vocal health (see Wellbeing) – how you use it, care for it, what you eat and drink.

Tip: Some things to avoid and tips to improve your vocal health (see Wellbeing)

- *Smoking* – avoid wherever possible; this has an impact on the quality of sound you make because smoking irritates and dehydrates the vocal folds. This can prevent the vocal folds from achieving closure and forces you to push too much air through the folds, causing them to dry out. Seek help and plan to give up smoking if you can.
- *Dehydration* – avoid this by staying hydrated, drinking water throughout the day. Drinking water or other fluids regularly enables your body to remain hydrated. Limit your alcohol and caffeine intake when possible. Try eating fruit when you drink as this is thought to help retain the hydration rather than flushing it through you.
- *Eating before sleep* – avoid eating directly before you lie horizontally and fall asleep. Enable time for your digestion to begin working before you require your body to engage in the process of sleep, particularly if you eat spicy or rich foods as this can trigger reflux – where the gastric acid from your stomach travels up the oesophagus causing a bitter taste and producing a heartburn sensation. This can cause a sore throat and in extreme cases you may lose your voice. Repeated vomiting from conditions such as norovirus or bulimia will also negatively impact your vocal folds. Eat earlier in the day and seek help from your doctor if you are unwell.
- *Shouting or screaming above noise* – at clubs or gigs with loud music, you are pushed to force your voice to be heard above it. This can have a damaging impact on your vocal folds and lead to voice loss or with extreme repetition create polyps or nodules. Either avoid the need to speak in these situations by dancing or using sign language or try to avoid them!

For the actor, losing your voice can mean losing your job. The sounds your voice make are shared through your mouth as a vessel; this happens alongside other activities: drinking, eating, playing an instrument and so on. There is therefore a lot of activity in this space, and it needs to be treated with care.

VOICE

- Your voice is unique, celebrate your sounds and retain authenticity.
- Explore vocal possibilities freely – vocal flexibility enables transformation.
- Your body unlocks your voice – release tension and release your voice.
- Vocal development utilises imagination and is not simply technical.
- Microphone technique – practice is experience.
- Protect your vocal health – demonstrate self-care.
- Breathe.

CHAPTER ELEVEN

Movement

Movement is an intrinsic part of your means of communication and as an actor you draw imaginatively upon your physical resources to fulfil your role as storyteller (see Imagination). The body holds intelligence and intuition which manifests through physical impulses. Exercises which focus on your instinctive impulses are so helpful in enabling you to trust your body to *know*. A shoal of fish streaming through the ocean or a starling murmuration manages to remain equidistant and in tune with each other – this is not the result of planning or following a leader but of connected body impulses. We too have this ability to go with the flow and trust our impulses. When we tune into the energy in a room with others, we can effortlessly move through space together with others in a group (known as flocking) or move independently and yet in harmony simultaneously. It is in our nature.

Physical training

Training your movement is about freeing up your impulses so they become clear and you can trust them as a default. Listening with your body involves its entirety and importantly this includes your organs, their systems, and your breath. The process of training the body involves building your physical strength and stamina, developing your agility including your coordination and flexibility, enabling you to find a flow and, as referred to in martial arts, 'to achieve maximum efficiency with minimum effort'. It also requires you to relinquish your mental tension so that the mind and body can be synchronised. To achieve such ease takes a lot of practice and there is a lot you can do independently to help your body. Ease will also help to free your voice and you are at your best when both body and voice are free (see Voice).

Warming up is crucial for any physical work; not only will it help you to avoid injury, but it will also enable you to push yourself further in any exercise. Your physical fitness (see Wellbeing) is important and inevitably dictates what you can achieve, so engaging in cardio and resistance activities are a good basis for maintaining your body and preparing it for work. Placing too much focus on building muscle will work against your aims as an actor. It can make you too rigid and bound when you are looking for flexibility and flow. So rather than spending time in the gym you may prefer to swim, play a team sport or cycle. It is also useful to study the anatomy of the body to fully appreciate its structure. This can enable you to experience its sensations more fully and to closely observe how your body works.

To work on your energy flow, it will help you to try activities such as Qi Gong, Tai Chi or Yoga which can really help to connect you with your body, generate energy, connect your breathing and develop mindfulness. Yoga will also help you to build strength, flexibility and stamina through stretching, using your core muscles and by retaining poses. Sequences in yoga and particularly in the Vinyasa Flow practice can also introduce you to a sense of movement flow and a new movement language. When you are stretching, release your breath and this will encourage the body to free up from unnecessary tension. Flexibility can also be developed through massage; create a habit of massaging your feet and body and if finances allow, treat your body with a professional massage.

Dancing is invaluable to develop your joy in expressivity, stamina, coordination and physical freedom. All actors will be asked at some point in their career to dance, whether that is choreographed or free style. The line between where movement ends and dance begins is a blurry one and it is not useful to separate them – rather it helps to embrace everything in this active scope as part of a whole. Free exercise such as playing, rolling down a hill or any free-flow activity will help to liberate your body and give it courage. Free running or parkour are also exciting ways to incorporate coordination, balance, agility and freedom.

Once the body is responsive and free, there are a range of approaches to movement which can give you a framework for developing your characterisations or a source for devising and creating play. The Japanese actor, Yoshi Oida, places his interest in the actor's impact on story and their skills in radiating energy. His book *The Invisible Actor* is a masterclass, full of analogies rather than hard and fast rules for acting – all aimed at enabling you to spark the imagination of the audience and for your skills to appear invisible.

Post-World War II, the choreographer Rudolph Laban developed key insights for the actor, identifying components of weight, time and space as a framework to explore his so-called *efforts*: floating, dabbing, wringing, thrusting, pressing, flicking, slashing and gliding. This work can bring great improvisational opportunities but also allow the actor to pay attention to detail and avoid physical generalisations. Much is written on this system of codifying movement, but if you can access an in-person workshop it will prove invaluable.

A system that can complement or be an alternative to this work is Anne Bogart's *viewpoints*, originally inspired by choreographer Mary Overlie and later developed by Bogart and Tina Landau. Nine categories or *viewpoints* in the system are held under two headings:

- Time – Tempo, Duration, Kinaesthetic Response, Repetition

- Space – Shape, Gesture, Spatial Relationship, Architecture, Topography.

A series of group exercises branch from this starting point and the aim is to develop an ensemble-led way of developing movement without allowing any of these viewpoints to lead a hierarchy. Movement tempo is linked to emotion, we cannot escape our heartbeat in our connection to tempo.

The work of Tadashi Suzuki, the Japanese theatre director, also brings an approach for the actor which will benefit their stamina, resilience, impulses, connection and personal discipline. The starting point is a consideration of the actor's centre of gravity in relation to a point beyond the audience. He is known most widely perhaps for his stomping sequences which draw on Japanese Kabuki, Indian Katakhali and Native American rituals. However, his work more widely involves statue poses and has a parallel to Laban with a focus on specific gestures and their itemisation. His interest in foot position and 'waking up the spirit' through stomping enables the actor to explore connection. His body poses and gestures inspire the voice to derive from the choices of the body. Suzuki gives the actor an embodied experience of potential action: an energy source and physical specificity to act or react.

Animal work is a fundamental part of actor training at drama school and has been developed in multiple ways throughout the decades. By observing animal behaviour and movement in detail, the actor begins to find connection to movement patterns, tempo, physical expression and habit outside of their own personal vocabulary. It proves to be a useful way of experimenting with character invention or in recognising what animal is most connected to a character's behaviour and therefore able to utilise elements of its movement. By observing animals both live and on film (so you can pause and replay) you will see the detail of their movement and behaviours very clearly. Putting these into your own body can be a fun and very creative opportunity. This is valuable for work on transformation and brings spontaneous life to behavioural choices (see Character). It is also work that you can lead yourself without reliance on a group.

Tip: Experiment with how your choice of animal may help character transformation.

- Consider your full execution of the animal as a 10 and fully commit.
- Slowly dial down from 10 to 5, allowing the character to appear with animal expressions.
- Dial down to 0 and then begin to dial up again to notice which elements of the animal come through, when and how they inform your character physicality.
- Find hooks from this work to help trigger your physical choices.

The elements – earth, fire, air and water – are also extremely helpful as a starting point for expressive movement and for discovering character physicality and movement (see Character). It opens your expressive range and stimulates your imagination (see Imagination) by initiating spontaneous improvisation. Each of these elements exists in a variety of forms. For example, fire can be a lit match, an open fire, a towering inferno, or a forest fire, each of which will create difference in terms of sensation and expression. These experiments can be self-led and specific to your character choices.

It can also be helpful to use colours to prompt character discovery and experimenting with your body response to colour can explore your emotional connection, allowing you a wide palette to work from and experiment with. Our Head of Movement asks students to consider head, heart, gut, groin as a framework for their acting impulses, which again allows for some lovely specificity in the work. Many practitioners will draw on the work of Jacques Lecoq, which identifies the 'seven states of tension' as a starting point and which other practitioners have since developed:

1 Exhausted – no tension at all in the body, an effort to speak.
2 Laid back – relaxed, easy, casual.
3 Neutral – totally present, ready for something to happen.
4 Alert – curious, indecisive.
5 Suspense – reactive, a disaster about to happen, tension between the eyes.
6 Passionate – tension explodes from the body, difficult to control.
7 Tragic – body is locked in solid tension.

> Tip: Experiment with each of these rising states of tension creating scenarios for each to awake the imagination. One to four are most likely to be seen in our everyday states.

Contact improvisation is used to develop an actor's experience of play and is incredibly freeing. Interacting in continuous motion with space and other actors, it invites you to explore, often in partner work at first, the relationship between your body and another. It explores awareness of movement, touch and sharing weight. It helps you to grow awareness of your own body and to collaborate sensitively with others. Capoeira is also helpful enabling you to combine partner work, acrobatics, and musicality in a martial art. African–Brazilian in origin it gives a good improvisational workout for your balance, flexibility and impulses. Physical improvisations with percussion can be used very successfully to unite a group of actors in movement and rhythm, and in creating a sense of ritual and ancient instinct – this connection is an uplifting experience.

There are more approaches to movement than can be offered here in a single chapter. All of them offer the actor a wealth of ideas to try, to consider and to experiment with. You are looking for approaches *you* can connect to, which make instinctive sense to *you*. Following any of these in a dutiful way will not bring you the results you want. You use your body every day, your body is unique to you and therefore exceptional. Listen to your body and find the ways to develop your physical skills that will bring you the most joy.

Presence

Your energetic presence is what is felt by an audience (see Connection). High energetic presence is charismatic, it draws us in like a magnet, we cannot stop watching, our entire being is attracted. Across cultures there is difference in terms of the focus placed on generating charismatic presence. Performances in Japan, India and Indonesia, for example, place focus on the eyes, hands and feet as the main transmitters of energy, communication and expression.

Historically, across the Asian and African continents, traditions of theatre to a degree have prioritised the body over the spoken word, making text more of an accompaniment to gesture and action. This heightens the need for charismatic presence and perhaps explains the impact of some of this work. The traditions of storytelling worldwide were not simply oral (see Imagination) but richly physical, utilising music to connect the heartbeat. It is important for Western actors in a time of globalisation to remember that Eurocentric traditions are not world traditions. With actors more able to work interculturally it is also important that we understand the differences between artistic collaboration versus cultural appropriation. We must be open to giving, collaborating and understanding rather than taking and claiming.

Energetic presence is a universally recognised element of performance and is a uniting factor in our desire to enjoy performance. It is radiated by the actor connecting to a sensation of the body, being present and alive in space and aware of gravity holding them. At one time practitioners talked about imagining roots and the sensation of being joined to the earth to achieve grounding. In more recent times it has become clearer that the body has more potential if it simply becomes conscious of gravity rather than trying to feel weighed down or 'planted'.

Tip: Explore radiating your kinosphere:

- Stand with space around you so you can reach out to your arm's length diameter.
- Relax your feet, release your breath, and let gravity support you.
- Explore the immediate space around you – your kinosphere – the space above and surrounding you is all part of your 360° energy field.
- Breath into this space and imagine you are creating a spherical air ball with you at its centre.
- Imagine this air ball in a colour, so it is lively or imposing.
- Ensure you are open energetically (see Wellbeing) and pour your energy source into the sphere.

Think of moments when you have beamed with pride or felt the sensation of attraction across a room – these are energetic experiences. You are looking to send your energetic field out beyond yourself, when it mixes with the kinosphere of another actor chemistry can amplify the sensations for you and for the audience. Energy sources are named differently in different cultures; for example, the hara is the Japanese word for belly and also means true nature, dantian means energy source in China and whilst there are three of these – head, chest and abdomen – it is the lower dantian which is the feed source to the other two. In the West we tend to refer to the gut as our emotional energy centre. Beliefs differ but it is undisputed that we have a source of energy production. It is also accepted that we produce an electromagnetic field, sometimes known as a 'universal light field' and our energy is impacted by other people and other energy sources. We are therefore also able to impact the energy of other actors.

Chakra systems are many, though it is believed they originated in India as part of the Hindu belief system over four thousand years ago. Typically, there are seven chakras in total (can be cited as four or twelve depending on the energy system) and they are traced to Maya Indians, Inca Indians of Peru, the Cherokee Indians of North America, China and Egypt who learnt from African traditions (see Wellbeing). Historical belief is rich and continues to be handed down through different lineages. For the actor, placing focus on a particular chakra can be a very useful tool for centring your energy.

To instigate your energy, you can use the exercises learnt from Qi Gong, Tai Chi or Yoga. You can also lift your energy radiation by tapping the whole body using cupped hands, or by clapping or rubbing your hands together for a prolonged period. To radiate your energy, it is helpful to imagine images of sending it out beyond your kinosphere. Use your breath to help you freely access the source of your energy and experience the channel of energy it helps you to find. Refer to your work on connection (see Connection), which helps to explain how energetic presence attracts others to you, whether that is your fellow actors or your audience.

Applied skills

The catch-all phrase 'physical theatre' is now a little tired and I suggest it is unhelpful to separate theatre in this way – all theatre is physical if the body is appearing in space. However, there are elements of movement work that are practised specifically to apply them to a style or form of theatre. These include but are not limited to dance, mask work, circus skills (balance, coordination, strength, agility and ariel work) and mime (physical acting without words). Stylised approaches to movement with or without text often cross dance boundaries. You may discover a particular flair for one or more of these elements and they are all useful strings to your bow. It is helpful to understand the history of each of these skills, for example, looking up commedia dell'arte to get more context on mask and physical comedy work.

Go and see physical work and as many movement styles as you can. Research the work of companies where you live, see their work, and imagine you are in the performance to get a sense of the skills you see. There are also other more technical areas which enable you to directly apply movement skills. Stage combat is a useful skill and most theatre work will require you to work with a fight director at some point in your career. Having a basic grounding in stage combat allows you to feel confident when working with a fight director. For combat or violence on film, a stunt double is sometimes employed but experience of combat is important. For any animated roles, motion capture is a skill you will employ for screen work, and which is now widely used. Wearing state-of-the-art equipment you record patterns of movement digitally; this is often used to bring life to an animated character for film or gaming. On screen the actor also needs to have an awareness of their physical choices and be able to repeat and synchronise this for physical continuity (see Space).

Whichever way you engage with movement work, when you are feeling blocked, the key to unlocking the answers you need is nearly always to engage in a physical exploration. It is movement that helps us to discover, to memorise and release our creative selves.

MOVEMENT

- Movement creates a language.
- Your body holds intelligence and intuition – listen to it.
- Ease of movement is your goal – release tension.
- Dancing, rolling, free running – practise the joy of waking up the spirit.
- Fitness is important to enable energy flow.
- Frameworks that codify movement or aid transformation are helpful.
- Creating sensations helps to generate energetic radiation.
- Motion capture will draw on physical skills including stage combat.

CHAPTER TWELVE

Space

The relationship of the actor to space is a fundamental one: in constructing the meaning of the work, for the technical creation of it and for the audience reception. The working requirements of the actor in space are different depending on the medium. Voice recorded media may require you to be alone in a sound booth or an acoustically treated space, which may be in your home or in a purpose-built studio. For radio drama you will usually do the recording sessions in a purpose-built studio with other actors. Screen work relies on studio sets and location spaces, which are both interior and exterior, and the space is defined by planned action, camera shots and angles. Exterior scenes rely heavily on the lighting and sound positions, which are high priority factors. Knowing your 'track' and 'hitting your mark' are essential for limiting the number of takes required and for the sake of continuity when you may have to repeat or continue action.

'Stage craft' and spatial awareness are essential for the actor. Perhaps better coined as 'space craft' to acknowledge that the stage is just one of many settings the actor may need to navigate. Performance spaces include a range of studio and mainstage theatres but also 'found sites' as used in site-specific or site-responsive work, outdoor stages or street theatre and temporary spaces such as festivals and pop-up venues. A television studio is also a space for performance and will occasionally facilitate a live audience. Film sets, location filming, motion capture with green screen set-ups, all require the actor to use their craft in navigating space and to take specific direction in space. Whether or not an audience is present in the space, these environments still require precision and spatial awareness (see Movement).

The power of space is tangible, a rehearsal room informs the resulting performance because that is where the creative decisions were made, and so the realisation of the work in the performance space carries traces of the rehearsal space. Space changes the quality of physical action and interaction and sets up an environment for the actor to engage in imaginatively. Size, geometry, floor quality or the acoustics of the spaces we inhabit inform our artistic, physical and vocal choices and our behaviours and relationship to the material and the project. A chilly church hall, a high-end purpose-built studio, a quirky repurposed room, an old gym, or a dusty warehouse – each of these spaces will have a different impact on the work you are making. Space and environment are *felt*, and their parameters contribute to the creative puzzle as you work through it.

Tip: In everyday life in different spaces, whether interior or exterior, imagine each of these spaces as a performance space.

- How does the space feel? What is the effect of a limitless horizon or a low ceiling?
- Try speaking a monologue or moving through your kinosphere (see Movement).
- Practise radiating your energy in each space to make it 'home'.

Look at bold architectural design such as the Turbine Hall at the Tate Modern in London or the Brooklyn Bridge in New York. How do these spaces speak to your imagination?

Even a touring set which you will rely on to remain constant will be housed in diverse spaces and the production can feel very different in each space it inhabits (see Process). Partly this is the physical architecture of the building which dictates the space, but the environment itself brings atmosphere in its shape, colour, texture, heritage and resources. There will be new logistics to encounter which are specific to the theatre you are touring to: longer or

shorter entrances depending on the geometry of the space, whether
the run around is uninterrupted, the position of dressing rooms,
configuration of the auditorium and aisle positions and so on. As
soon as you have the go-ahead from your Stage Manager, always
move through your track in each new space you encounter to avoid
surprises. Actors need to quickly be at home with anything new.

Mise en scène

The *mise en scène* means *to place on stage*. It is a term considered in
the making of work both for screen and stage. On screen, the curation
of what is placed on 'stage' is deliberate. The spatial relationship
of objects to each other is meticulously orchestrated; their use
by actors, the movement around them, camera shots, angles and the
choices made in the edit, are all carefully constructed. The resulting
picture will serve the vision of the filmmaker and producers and
impact the way in which the story is told for an audience and from
which character's perspective. The narrative perspective, ability
to cut between locations, close-ups, wide angles and panoramas
to support the action – all this is the power of filmmaking.

The stage picture in theatre is also deliberate, yet gives its
audience more freedom to consider the *mise en scène,* to choose
perspective and to see beyond the focussed action. Theatre has less
manipulative power in terms of the directed 'gaze' of screen media.
In theatre the *mise en scène* will include the whole picture for much
of an audience's experience and so the skill of the theatre maker is
to move the eye of the audience without changing the picture so
often. Lighting, sound, integrated film, movement, flying scenery
and scene changes – all of these add to the picture, move it or swipe
it clean. The stage picture in theatre is usually achieved in a more
collaborative fashion through rehearsals, with creatives making
more equal contributions, guided by the director. Acting choices
you make in the space involving movement and the use of props
will enable the *mise en scène* to evolve during rehearsals.

Your job is to understand the picture and your part in it, both
stylistically and technically. Your use of space in any visual medium
will be a part of the *mise en scène* and so it will tell the collective
story and not simply that of your character. In site-specific theatre,
the space itself evokes narrative, the placing of objects and actors is

relational and helps to steer this. In a dance piece on an empty stage, the awareness of the *mise en scène* is entirely heightened because it is reliant on the dancer's relationship to space. All performance work is seen in relation to space.

The role of the audience is to watch the space and what is in it; you must always assume your audience can see everything you do on stage unless there are viewing restrictions. They see every element so if during a scene you drop a prop, a piece of costume or a running prop such as food, the audience will watch it until you have picked it up. Use your spontaneous impulse to notice and retrieve it rather than 'pretending' it isn't there – if you can see it, they can see it. A prop left on stage may end up there for a series of scenes and it will entirely pull focus, steal the action and even create narrative!

Proxemics

At the onset of the Coronavirus pandemic in 2020, there was a new and global awareness of our proximity to each other because of imposed social distancing restrictions. We began to see the value of space freshly and to test our own sense of measuring it. Proxemics is the deliberate use of space to separate people, objects or fixed obstacles. The actor can use proxemics to create meaning, atmosphere, suspense and emotional response. It is a powerful tool and often underutilised by actors in rehearsal because they perceive spatial relationships to be the domain of the director. In the same way, 'blocking' – dictating the position and travel of the actor in each moment – is still largely attributed to the role of the director.

The theory of proxemics, largely defined in the 1960s by anthropologist, Edward Hall, is useful not only for theatre makers but also for the actor. His fundamental idea was that there are four types of distance that people choose to keep: intimate, personal, social and public and he quantified these by distance and territory. He looked at the effects of population density on behaviour, communication and social interaction and it is interesting for us to consider this work.

In relation to character, you can use it to explore connection, which is informed by your spatial distance (see Connection).

The physical distance between characters indicates the type of relationship they have and the situation they are in. The function and purpose of the space defines territorial boundaries and will inform proxemic choices, albeit in an enforced way. Body angles, touch and eye contact further reveal the familiarity that exists between characters. Using Hall's distances, which are chosen rather than enforced by circumstances, we have multiple opportunities to experiment with choices and their visual meaning:

Distance	Measurement	Logistics	Experience
Intimate	0 to 18 inches	may involve touch and body contact	sensual
Personal	18 inches to 4 feet	confidential interaction, eye contact	heart
Social	4 to 10 feet	peripheral vision, engaged, energetic	sensory
Public	over 10 feet	spatially aware, full freedom	exposed

Experimenting with these distances can inform your character relationships and choices; for example, if you are in intimate proximity you may choose to be more subtle in your choices than in public proximity. However, if you are feeling territorial your choices may be bolder. Territory is important to consider for the actor, all space is perceived to be owned and the character's relationship to that ownership will dictate how comfortable they feel in that space. Home, living space of friend or family, vehicle, school, church, office, park, shop, hospital, forest and so on. Understanding the impact of the environment on your character and the reason for being there will help to inform your proxemic choices. Experience how the breath is impacted differently at each of these specific distances in different situations and how that may influence your choices.

Observing proxemic behaviours in everyday situations is a valuable part of character study (see Character). The detail you can gain from observation of behaviour is so valuable; notice how people respond when someone enters their territory or moves closer to them. Your observation together with your imagination and the director's vision can produce magic. In different cultures people have different perceptions and beliefs of what constitutes personal space. This includes how close it is acceptable to stand to people, based on whether they are strangers, acquaintances, family, friends or loved ones. In your research it is important to factor in cultural understanding and allow it to help you make authentic choices (see Context).

There is no single way of directing actors or of running a rehearsal room, nor is there a right or a wrong way. You can bring your independence to rehearsals by exploring possible proxemic possibilities in the work and your director then has a choice to engage in further exploration of these. Even a director who intentionally dictates the boundaries of space in the construction of the *mise en scène* may still be open to experiment with front-footed actors. If a director sets the proxemic relationship you have in space with other actors or objects in specific 'blocking', it will be your job to inhabit this and make sense of it. So, however you arrive at an understanding of your relationships in space and where you are going, you ultimately need to own your movement and proximity to other actors and objects.

On screen, the use of proxemics is largely manipulated by the camera, and it is the audience for whom this features the most. Audience proximity to the action is led by close-ups, panoramas, aerial shots and so on. They may witness an intimate scene at a distance or as part of it and may be distanced from more public proximity or zoomed into it. The actor must understand the technical needs of space during filming and the more they can understand what the camera set-up is, the more opportunities they may have to contribute to the action.

The industry is finally acknowledging the importance of support for actors when approaching intimate scenes with sexual content, and this is a positive development for actors in this century. It mirrors the way we have embraced specialist fight directors, who bring expertise to realise a director's vision safely and give confidence to the actors they work with. It is essential that we now create space for intimacy practitioners and the practical and mental health support this can bring you in rehearsal and on set. The breadth of this work includes scenes of both consensual sexual content and those of sexual violence.

It is important that you completely understand, when signing an acting contract, exactly what is required of you. If you are not prepared to take on nudity, for example, your agent must know this to avoid wasting your time and theirs. The decision is always *yours* and your reputation is not judged on whether you are prepared to take on nudity. It is possible you will be required to approach intimate scenes without nudity so make sure you read the script entirely and with care before you agree to any part. Ask your agent to enquire if an intimacy coordinator will be contracted and persist in requesting one if this has not been factored in. By working with boundaries and support you are protecting yourself from possible abuse, whether this is deliberate, unintentional or opportunistic – all are unacceptable. Valuing yourself needs to be a proactive decision on your part. Self-care is essential and only you can implement this and safeguard against any negative impact on you (see Wellbeing).

Audience

The simplicity for the actor of being in a space and telling a story to an audience can be liberating, removing the reliance on production values, and placing focus on performance (see Imagination). Peter Brook, over half a century ago in his seminal book *The Empty Space*, explored this, finding the root of *why* we are in the space and *what* we are doing there. All spaces hold an energy and, when actors share the space with each other and an audience, the combined energies create atmosphere. It is that atmosphere which keeps live performance going – we forget that at our peril (see Process).

Depending on the style of the production and the writing you may have direct communication with the audience (see Text). Pantomime, for example, involves direct interaction with the audience and embraces the auditorium space – this is designed to share the experience and create a united purpose. Metatheatre – theatre which references theatre and the unfolding theatrical event – has become more popular in this century, with the audience in on the concept and being reminded that they are viewing a theatrical conceit. This creates a shared ownership of the event between actors and audience and invites a level of intellectual observation rather than asking for audience immersion. At times metatheatre combines elements of knowing with moments of immersion and then returns to its theatrically conscious convention to manipulate the audience experience.

Many plays also use direct address with characters speaking straight to the audience. This is referred to as breaking the 'fourth wall'. The fourth wall was a concept born in the nineteenth century and described the theatrical convention of an audience watching the action of a play – typically through a drawing room wall – whilst the actors were unaware of their presence and a 'fourth wall' was imagined. Stanislavski in his advice to actors referred to this practice as 'public solitude' and, throughout the modern period, this use of naturalism was so much in fashion in European theatre it was hard for them to imagine any other theatre style had ever existed. The space between the audience and the actors appeared to be of no consequence, they existed as if the audience were not there. The actors would behave as if in private, despite being watched intently. Television dramas continued this convention, and the British 'kitchen sink drama' was the form in which we became accustomed to watching the lives of others almost as a voyeur. Naturalism had given way to a social realism, both in theatre and television.

Breaking the fourth wall, or in television and film 'breaking the screen', has become much more usual in the twenty-first century. The interaction with the audience does not need to be verbal. Indeed, Phoebe Waller-Bridge gave us a masterclass in her television series *Fleabag* where she, as the protagonist, regularly looks to the audience and makes non-verbal remarks on her own behaviour or on the action. Our current stylistic tastes are closer to those of the Elizabethan age where we would expect 'in-jokes' with an audience, asides and soliloquys written into the event. Theatre traditions across the world have long made the audience the most important element of the shared experience, placing an emphasis on the importance of the live event. Without an audience, a performance does not exist.

The writer having direct communication with the audience and using the actor as a vessel reminds us that we are in an imaginative world, a construct. In South American forum-style theatre, Augusto Boal has shown that direct address and audience awareness is particularly useful as a convention for political or social-justice focussed work. Forum Theatre identifies a need for change and offers liberation to the oppressed through a form of social activism. The role of the audience as jury was epitomised by Bertholt Brecht's work in the early twentieth century, another form of activating the audience to recognise a need for societal change.

In site-specific work, the audience is usually in a non-theatre space and will draw personal associations to the space based on their life experiences. For example, if the performance takes place in a disused playground, it is likely to evoke childhood, teenage or parental memories. The actor's work in this space will be read by an audience through a lens which is very specific to them. Different staging and audience configurations also make an enormous impact on the space, changing the position of the action, how close the audience are to the actors and to what extent the set design is expressionistic. The main stage configurations you will encounter are:

1   End-on or proscenium arch
    The audience face in a single direction to watch the action. Action is contained within the box of the playing space using exits stage left and right, both upstage and downstage through tabs into the wings. An end-on studio space can be more open and immediate than a theatre with a proscenium arch, which is framed. The greater depth in the space, the more work is required to ensure you vocally project your sound to the auditorium.

2   Thrust or on three sides
    In this configuration the stage extends beyond the apron at the font of the space and pushes into the audience. This enables an audience to feel closer to the action by surrounding it on three sides. Careful staging is required, and it can help to create more dynamic movement. The audience are aware of each other as well as the actors.

3   In the round
    This configuration dispenses with conventional sets entirely and gives the most imaginative freedom in the realisation of the work. Usually offering the actors four exits, the audience surround the action completely and are close to the action. In this configuration, actors must be connected to their physical power in the space in terms of stage craft and presence as

they will always have their back to a part of the audience. The audience can see each other during the performance and can feed off each other.

4 Traverse
    In traverse, the audience sit opposite each other, usually on the long side of a studio space and the actors travel the action through this space. This often plays out like a tennis match for the audience who watch to their left and right until action lands in front of them. Sets are usually minimal in this configuration, placing focus on the two ends rather than the space in which you traverse. The actor must work hard to ensure that all the audience can see and hear the action.

You can only make decisions in the space when you understand what the space represents for the audience and whether stylistically you are required to see the audience.

SPACE

- 'Space craft' each medium requires a different use of space.
- Space and environment are felt.
- Stage picture – *mise en scène* – is impacted by your choices.
- Proxemics can create meaning, atmosphere, suspense and emotional response.
- Treat space as your home rather than owned by the director.
- Intimacy practice is an important development for actors.
- Audiences share space with you and their space configuration changes your relationship with them.

CHAPTER THIRTEEN

Practice and Beyond

Training can help shape your career trajectory and is a wonderful opportunity to place focus on your development, but it is not a guarantee of a career. Your future journey will be shaped by a mixture of the opportunities available, your casting match, your skillset, serendipity, networking, life choices, some degree of design, and all in conversation with your agent if you have one. Actors are very often employed by directors or creative teams they have previously worked with. Invest your time in developing your skills – the higher the level you can deliver them at, the more likely you are of achieving re-employment when a suitable role is available. Ultimately, it is easier to employ a great company member who is skilled and sufficiently independent to offer ideas and take responsibility for their work. The trend to consider an actor's social media profile and count their followers as a means of guaranteeing their suitability for a role is sad but true. Like most trends, it may be best ignored and is by no means a universal measure. Commit to networking and being out in the world but focus on your *development* and what you have to offer.

There will come a point at which you know you have a personal working method – a practice. Your practice is your ally, it will stand with you and advocate for you, enable you to believe in your work. You will be able to confidently practise, keep up your interaction with your skills and continue to develop them. You will also feel confident in the skills you are taking into a job or the rehearsal room. You will rely on your preparation more than anything once you begin to work and it will always support you to access your practice (see Process). Your working method will adapt and modify as you grow your experience. It is important to know that you are everything you need – an independent actor, with skills on a journey. Believe.

Culture has a significant impact on our attitude to practising. In the West, practising can be considered as a chore – wanting immediate results you try to avoid the painful process of getting it 'wrong'. Yet, to get it 'right' you usually need to have experienced getting it 'wrong'. As a generalisation, in the East there appears to be less aversion to practising – indeed, it is a powerful and positive act which will develop you over a lifetime rather than one fuelled by a fear of failure (see Fear).

I have observed the practice of many actors during my career and in various contrasting scenarios. In Beijing, China I witnessed student actors engaging in self-led practice at the crack of dawn and wholly cherishing the opportunity. In Ljubljana, Slovenia the actors I met were more interested in practising as a collective, relishing the spontaneity generated when working together. In Hanoi, Vietnamese performer puppeteers at the Water Theatre appeared religious in their commitment, apparently devoting long hours to their practice, and mainly performing for free. The drive and enthusiasm I have been met with by North American actors in relation to their practice is always inspiring and of course in the United States there is an embedded culture of actors continuing 'class' as part of their ongoing learning long after graduation.

Malcolm Gladwell popularised Swedish psychologist Anders Ericcson's theory that it takes 10,000 hours to master your craft. The theory, which was later rejected, explored effort versus IQ and was hugely appealing as it presented a 'formula for success'. However, there remains an element of reliability in the assertion that effective practice can improve your skills (see Process). Practice alone cannot be everything; being curious, committed and being prepared to take courage are very much at the heart of your learning journey. Being open to learning every day is the greatest challenge you can set yourself, understanding that none of us can ever know everything. Ericcson proposed that 'deliberate practice' is a key to improvement and that working outside of your comfort zone is important.

Tip: Regular, deliberate, effective – common sense approach to practising.

Regular – Make a regular commitment, daily if possible and at least weekly so you can evaluate your progress. What is your best time of day for learning? Allow a pattern to emerge before changing to a different cycle. Try to practise at the same time so you are easily able to compare your work and energy levels. In the first instance it is better to under commit and succeed than to over commit and cancel your plan. Like any new plan you must be realistic about your available time, or you will not manage it and ultimately give up.

Deliberate – Focus on what requires attention, practising for hours in a general and unfocussed way will not reap rewards. Specificity is everything. The results may well remain the same if you do not change what you are doing. Equally, if you overload yourself with new information, then your mind and body will struggle to process it. Quantity does not equate with quality. What resources and time do you *need*? What will you practice – warm-up sequences, accent work, movement exercises, application of text exercises, character work, sight-reading? If you have not learnt a text securely, it wastes your time trying to apply exercises to it.

Effective – How will you practice? Simply repeating a monologue a dozen times is not effective, you will find no difference other than delivery speed! You are aiming to retain skill level previously achieved and to improve upon it. Identify the current hurdles in your delivery of a monologue, for example:

- sections where you are not making sense of the line
- transitions from one unit to the next
- building to the event or highest dramatic point
- comedic punchlines – landing the joke
- first unit and last unit.

If you are practising a warm-up sequence, take each element in turn before linking the sequence together. Once it is linked together go back and look at the transition between each element. This is the same principle as practising a dance sequence – drill down to the specificity of each move or position before attempting to put it back together.

Try to lower the stakes when you are practising; it does not matter if you do not get it first time, perseverance reaps rewards and can be a real boost to the confidence. When you practise you are building proficiency, which is linked to fear – when we practise something we are less proficient at, we fear seeing our limitations and it can knock our confidence (see Wellbeing). If you are physically injured be mindful and exercise self-care, change your practice list and do not return to physical work until you have healed, and it is safe to do so.

The point of honing your skills is so they become embedded as part of your physical habit or verbal lexicon. Once you have regularly practised your skills many of these will become automatic and you will employ them like muscles as if they are second nature. It can be daunting when putting all your new knowledge, understanding and practice together, to make sense of it. Creating the habit of practising will help with this and requires you to be organised. Write it in your schedule either digitally or by hand and give yourself reminders (see Training). Choose it as the only 'non-negotiable' on your schedule. If you are working in numerous freelance capacities or have dependants and complex draws on your time, a timetable of activity can help you to achieve your goals. Fix times when you are committing to your own continued development and practice – take yourself seriously.

If you are on a self-led approach you may choose to promote yourself in a showcase when you feel ready. Take time to research agents, casting directors and other industry professionals and ensure you target them specifically. Persevere with your communications and ensure you have promoted the event and built a list of confirmed attendees. Make use of your networks and ask people to help you. People are kind and willing to help if they know what you need. Try not to place too much expectation on this sort of event; it is a useful platform to share your work and attract interest, but it is unlikely to bring about any sort of 'big break'. Record your work and send it electronically too; increasingly this is more popular – it can even help to send extracts in advance to persuade people to attend in person.

We often refer to an actor's toolbox – the image is useful to illustrate the need for a range of different tools that you can use to apply in a range of contexts. Sifting through your journal to create a list of the elements in your toolkit can give you a great reminder of the work you have engaged in – use it as a checklist when you are working on a role (see Process). This can help when you are feeling blocked and need to unpick your choices, and prevents you from relying solely on external feedback. You will usually know if something is not working because you feel it, and whilst of course you will get creative feedback from the director, be independent and not reliant.

Example list of tools for exploration and finding new solutions:

Tools to use	Action taken	Results	Follow up
Units and objectives	• Identified units and marked them • Identified objectives for each unit • Tried playing each unit objective	Narrative became clearer but some objectives are not clear	Change some objectives Find actions to play to help hone the purpose of the text
Animal work	• Chose to observe a gazelle on film • Experimented with detailed movement	Character more connected and physically embodied but energy is pushing the spoken tempo	Experiment with age (e.g. arthritis), or a reason to slow the pace Try a vocal tactic to help balance this – stretching vowels to slow down
Colour	• Character feels yellow – improvised physically to explore yellow sensations	Makes the character feel too light	Explore orange to find more grounding

The examples in the table show that the results of one action often lead you on to explore another tool. The entries in this table can become infinite. This is because all the actor's work is interconnected and holistic. A physical choice will impact a vocal choice which may reinterpret text and change meaning. Changed meaning will impact the intention and that in turn will impact the purpose of speaking and therefore the action being played towards another actor. The links are infinite and provide you with so much opportunity to explore depth and discover creative solutions. Once you move into performance mode, this work will be in the background and released from your consciousness (see Process). You can only do one thing at a time.

Sometimes on set or in a recording booth you may need to make a quick new decision that does not have the benefit of this rigorous exploration. In those instances, you will make good decisions based on your training, existing or developing practice and your instinct. Never doubt these decisions – make choices and commit entirely to them. This is an example of when you need to utilise your mental strength, take courage and trust in yourself.

So, at what point can you call yourself an actor? If you are dedicating your time to the pursuit of acting work, then you are an actor – you do not need to seek permission. It is not about your status in relation to agents, unions, training institutions or the size of your résumé. Everyone starts somewhere. It is your occupation whether you are actively working on a specific role or not. The bits in between 'acting' are as much a part of the job – responding to or creating opportunities and expanding your network.

People are fascinated by actors and as soon as you declare yourself to be one you will be asked, *'have I seen you in anything?'*, *'do you know anyone famous?'*, *'what are you in at the moment?'* and when they do see you in something, *'what is next?'*. Do not be annoyed. The questions always come from a place of innocence, fascination or genuine interest. They may be the wrong questions for *you* but they are well intentioned. Whilst they can feel like an attack on your success as an actor, they are in fact confirmation that you are being *accepted* by them as an actor. Spend a moment figuring out a response to these questions, so you do not feel triggered when you get asked them and can reply easily. Humour is a wonderful tool and can move the conversation on without awkwardness; however, do ensure you are not self-deprecating. You have struggled to get to a place where you accept yourself as an actor – do not undermine yourself now.

The different types of work for actors in the creative industries have become extensive. If you pursue representation by an agent, you will be asked what sort of work you see yourself doing. Remember that it is important to answer that question honestly, being aware of the wealth of options available to you is essential so you can imagine yourself in a variety of contexts. Asserting your independence in pursuit of what you want is essential throughout your career and what you want will change with time and experience. It is entirely in your gift to change your mind. Your agent can give you a clear picture of the types of opportunities they deal with. Never say never. Be open to all opportunities before ruling them out because of experience or preference. Our greatest fear can sometimes result in revealing our greatest success.

The theatre landscape became more precarious following the Coronavirus pandemic when actors faced cancelled contracts and reduced audiences. However, whilst theatre is still struggling, there are so many new opportunities being created from streaming channels who are making new content all year round. Voiceover for audiobooks, animation films and voicing for the gaming industry have also become a booming marketplace and actors are increasingly relying on it for their incomes. Indeed, many actors have built their own home studios in cupboards and sheds to be able to deliver on a variety of recorded media contracts. You may not have the space or finance to do this currently but putting it on the wish list is a positive move.

Learn how the industry works and your role within it; there are many resources to help you with this. Take care, though – do not make being an actor purely about the business aspect or your imagination will fade, and you will lose the heart. Keep focussed on the development of your skills, learn on each job, keep a record of what you did. What results did you get? How would you approach a similar challenge next time? If you have not chosen a conservatoire-style training route you may be very appealing to those casting directors who are fascinated by what they see as the authenticity of the untrained actor. The search for authenticity in some genres of film is seen as difficult to replicate with trained actors. There are arguments that can be positioned in either direction, of course, but this is a trend that may continue.

Your reputation is formed every time you work with or meet other professionals. The creative industries have a very social network of professionals, and you will discover that everyone either knows someone you do or does so by very few degrees of separation. Never talk unkindly about anyone to anyone. If you do have those thoughts, find a moment to unpick the specifics of why you feel something and keep it to yourself; often these feelings are linked to fear. If you are booked for a job, turn up prepared. If you are booked for a casting, turn up prepared. If you are booked for a meeting, turn up. Unless you are unwell and you have communicated this immediately, there is no wriggle room on turning up. Reputation is something you can have some control over. A poor reputation is hard to recover from.

How do you conduct yourself in the professional environment? Are you reliable, punctual, ready to deliver, open to others, respectful and trusting, kind and generous? The independent actor is all of these and more because they afford themselves the agency and confidence to be this person. So, if you have done this work for yourself, be yourself (see Wellbeing). No one wants to work with a self-centred, unreliable, fearful and unkind actor full of attitude! Why would they? Ensure that you have the mental resilience and physical stamina to deliver a contract before you accept it. This is not only for your own welfare but for the actors and creatives you will work with. Be sure you will turn up to rehearsals and performances.

Whilst you will find yourself surrounded by some fantastic people – actors, creatives, wardrobe, stage management, technicians – it is wise not to rely on reassurance from them. Your confidence must be developed by you and your self-sufficiency will enable you to thrive. Of course, there will be support available for you in these working relationships, but also, develop your resilience so you are not reliant on them. Be a team player, be genuinely supportive of others and this will enable you to see beyond yourself, encouraging others to develop confidence and independence.

Finally, there are many more actors in the world than jobs to fill. If you are open to learning and to life you will not see this as a barrier to you (see Creativity). There will always be ways for you to work in this brilliant industry and it may be a combination of working for producers and producing work yourself. Perhaps you will develop as a multi-hyphenate and celebrate as a portfolio artist. Perhaps you are mid-career and refreshing your practice and goals. You cannot know what will happen when you are starting out, or in the space beyond, so enjoy going with the flow, embrace the unknown and thrive creatively.

CHAPTER FOURTEEN

Exercises for a Self-led Approach

The exercises in this chapter are self led. These exercises have no hierarchy and are offered up for you to decide their use to you personally. Millions of exercises exist in this field, many brilliant ones, which you will find through the resources in the following chapter and many more besides. The physical suggestions are not fixed: adapt the exercises to work with your own body. Record your discoveries in your journal.

Connection, movement

1 Shake out, include every part of your body and without pushing, allow any natural sounds to release as you shake. Next, take on stretches that your body feels it needs – listen to your body, what feels stiff or tired or tight?

2 Clap your hands continuously and place emphasis on your out breath. Keep clapping until your muscles begin to struggle with the repetition. Close your eyes and relax, notice the energetic sensation in your arms. Release your breath and open your eyes.

3 With your spine at full height, rotate your torso round to the left and then to the right to its comfortable reach. Allow your arms and hands to freely follow the momentum of the movement.

4   Let your arms swing and slowly accelerate your speed. As you move, your hands will naturally tap against your torso. This Qi Gong exercise helps to stimulate the nerves, tendons and muscles surrounding the shoulder. It also wakes up the energy in the body.

5   Gently return to stillness, then, cupping the hands, vigorously tap the body from your chest down and then up your body.

6   Notice the sensations in the body and remember how to recreate them.

Imagination, character

A range of stimuli, such as locations, objects and art can ignite 'play', and the opportunities are everywhere. Using imagery, sound, touch, taste and smell to stimulate associative stories is equally valuable and an important way to evoke the imagination.

1   Go to a coffee shop, train station or park and focus on the people you see.

2   Identify them as characters in a scene, invent their Ws, imagine their super objectives and their relationship to each other.

3   What could be the imagined drama in the scene? Look for clues to help your imagination. Choose one character and as a stream of consciousness speak or write their interior monologue.

4   Immerse in the idea of those words being spoken aloud to someone else in the scene and imagine how the scenario ends.

Connection, imagination, space

1   Lie on the floor in a comfortable position and in turn place awareness in each part of your body.

2   Move each body part momentarily as you place your awareness. Close your eyes and become aware of your breathing.

3   Each time you release your breath (exhale), imagine that your torso is opening, becoming wider, softer.

4   Imagine your breath is released from each part of your body in your favourite colour. This colour reaches out and beyond you, inviting your body into the space.

5   Open your eyes, roll onto your side and slowly come to your full height. Spend a minute relaxing to ensure you are placing your full weight evenly. Make the body soft in your joints to help you balance.

6   Repeat points 2–5 again but this time in the space and, keeping your eyes open, focus on a fixed point.

7   Close your eyes as you exhale this imaginary-coloured breath, see it reaching as far as your point of focus, then open your eyes.

8   Place your focus on an object or piece of furniture in the space and imagine as you breathe that you are creating a sphere of colour. Send the coloured air to reach out and fill your 360° kinosphere. Open your torso and embrace the energy.

Connection, space, movement

1   Be in a space where you can move freely without obstacles and where you feel emotionally safe.

2   Lie on the floor in a comfortable position and become aware of your heartbeat – find your pulse to easily access this connection. Close your eyes and focus on its rhythm and sensations.

3   Slowly begin to consider the position of each of the organs in your body and visualise them; consider the function they are performing without any direct conscious effort from you.

4   Create very gentle continuous movement in your body – such as rolling or rocking – and in turn gently see if you can experience the sensation of engaging each of these organs. Give yourself a lot of time to tune into the sensations.

5   Next, let your body lead on moving into positions that give you a joyful sensation.

6   As you experiment, open your eyes and give your body permission to move beyond the floor. Each time you find a joyful sensation, allow the body to repeat it. Ask '*what does my*

body want to do?' and follow through in granting each wish and embracing any movement impulses in the space.

7   Gently bring the exercise to an end when you feel that your exploration has naturally finished.

Connection, imagination, character

1   Place your focus on an object in the room. Look only at the object and move closer to encounter it.

2   Notice the shape, colour, feel, smell of it and consider the function it serves.

3   Imagine its history, how long has it existed, what has it meant in its lifetime and for whom?

4   As you fall deeper into communion with the object let your imagination create scenarios for the object or those who may have known it. Close your eyes.

5   Underscore your story with sound or music in your head and allow an emotional connection to it.

6   Sit with this for as long as you feel able to and then slowly come back into the space.

7   Now replace this object with one which is relevant for a character you are working on.

8   Repeat the exercise in character, discover the connection and create a character memory of this communion.

Voice, imagination

1   Lie comfortably on the floor and become aware of your breath.

2   Place your hands gently on your ribcage and let them rise and fall with each breath.

3   Breathe in through your nose and out through your mouth, notice the sensations you experience.

4   Imagine you are breathing in through your feet and become aware of the sensations this creates.

5 Lay your hands by your sides, palms facing upwards and imagine the breath coming through your hands. How does this differ from the sensation of breathing through the feet?

6 Slowly roll to one side and using your hands and knees come to standing.

7 Slowly move into the space experimenting with each of these in turn. How does it change the breath? How does it change your movement through the space?

Character, voice, imagination

1 Choose an animated film you have not watched before and put it on with the sound off.

2 Pick a character and imagine from the look and behaviours of the character what their vocal qualities and accent could be.

3 Write a short monologue for the character based on action in the film and experiment with vocal sounds and qualities to bring the character to life.

4 Record your voice.

5 Watch the animation with the sound on. What choices does the actor in the animation make?

6 How are they like your own choices? How do they differ? What can you adjust in your own choices?

Text, movement

1 Choose a monologue you are not familiar with.

2 Read it aloud and make instinctive decisions in pencil, sectioning it up into units/chunks.

3 Choose a movement for each chunk: skipping, sliding, running, hopping etc. and use the space to explore these simultaneously with the text.

4 Explore the changes of movement and adapt them to feel organic with the text, repeating until the right quality of movement feels right with each change.

5 Exaggerate the transitions and repeat until the body has ownership of each movement.

6 Speak the text without committing to movement but remaining connected to that exploration. The movement may reappear through gesture or create an internal sensation.

7 How has the text changed because of your movement?

Text, imagination

1 Choose a monologue or poem and three instrumental pieces contrasting in style and tempo.

2 Work on the text to discover its natural rhythms, paying attention to punctuation and phrasing.

3 Play each of the pieces of music in turn underneath your vocalisation of the text.

4 Encourage your body to respond to the impact of the music, allow the music to initiate movement or to change you vocally, exaggerate your responses so you can feel the full extent of their impact.

5 Vocalise the text without the music and become aware of what has changed. What new discoveries reveal themselves?

Text, context

Take a monologue you are unfamiliar with and observe its

1 Structure – observe paragraph length, sentence length, punctuation, dialect or vernacular, rhetorical questions.

2 Content – identify the narrative, choice of language and specific words, characters mentioned, topics revealed, personal information revealed, level of stakes.

3 Intention – ask: What is the impulse to speak? Why is the character telling this story or sharing these facts/truths/ reflections? Why are they sharing it now? How does the character hope to affect the person that they are telling? What does the character discover by speaking? What context is revealed?

4   Absorb your discoveries and then record yourself speaking the text. Playback and consider where you can better clarify meaning, raise the stakes or tell the story.

Space, context, creativity

1   Choose an interior or exterior space which you have access to.
2   Research the historical context including the people associated with it.
3   Spend time in the space, feel its parameters and soak up its atmosphere.
4   Imagine an event there, e.g., a pond where a group may come to sail toy boats; a car park where a car boot sale would run. In the space, write a stream of consciousness passage that imagines a dramatic happening at the event.
5   Review your writing and shape it from the perspective of one of the people you have researched.
6   Work on it as a monologue, perform it in the space, record it and reflect on it. Consider making a series.

Character, context

Choose a character to explore. If the character is a real person or historical figure you can engage in comprehensive research to complete the following task. Otherwise, if the facts in the script have been accounted for, your imagination and your own body are the limits for this exercise.

1   Use the framework of circumstances known in a play – either explicitly or implicitly – to map the journey of a character's body. Where you have no facts, invent them.
2   Start the journey in the womb and travel through to the age of the character in the script.

   ● What sort of pregnancy did the character's mother have? What was the birth like?

   ● Early years – were there any medical complications?

- As a child or teenager did they sustain any injuries?
- How did they use their body as a teenager?
- How nurturing were they of their body?
- Has the character tested their body with alcohol, drugs, sport, extreme adrenalin, self-harm?
- What work activities have they engaged in?
- How physically fit are they?
- Has the body had many adventures?
- What is their most comfortable gait?
- What is the quality of energy that consumes their body?

3 Record your discoveries and explore how this information can be a catalyst for your physical and behavioural choices.

Connection, voice, context

This is a voice journey research project.

1 Try to find out how you used your voice as a baby. Did you cry/scream a lot? What age were you when you started speaking? What were your first words? Were you a confident speaker? Whose voices were you learning from?

2 What memories do you have of your voice during your school years? Were you particularly vocal? Achievement at school is linked to how confident we may be to use our voice. Were you a student with their hand up successfully answering questions? Was your voice ignored at school, at home, in the playground? Did you feel that your voice was not worthy of being heard? Was your voice celebrated? Was your voice criticised?

3 What memories do you have of using your voice creatively or feeling free vocally? Reflect on moments of joy, laughter, singing, shouting – how does it feel when you use your voice spontaneously and emotionally? What natural volume do you feel confident using? How does your voice respond when you are sick? Do you have a history of losing your voice?

4 What feedback comments have friends, family, colleagues, students or strangers made about your voice, whether invited or otherwise? What words have been associated with your voice?

5 Gather audio recordings of the voices you grew up with – parents, guardians, siblings. These may already exist or you may record them now.

6 Look for any audio recordings you have of your own voice at different moments in your life (these may be on film). Then record yourself speaking now, ideally speaking freely and spontaneously or reading something you have written yourself so that you avoid 'correcting' yourself or using a more formal tone.

7 What words describe what you hear? Reflect on your connection to your voice and its journey so far.

CHAPTER FIFTEEN

Resources

You will find here an eclectic list of resources, which connect to the chapters in this book and its overarching theme of independence.

Acting

Alfreds, M. (2007) *Different Every Night*. London: Nick Hern Books.

Caldarone, M. (2004) *The Actor's Thesaurus*. London: Nick Hern Books.

Chekhov, M. (1993) *On the Technique of Acting*. New York: Harper Perennial.

Hagen, U. (2008) *Respect for Acting*. 2nd edition. Hoboken, NJ: Wiley.

Johnstone, K. (2018) *Impro*. London: Bloomsbury Academic.

Luckett, S. (2016) *Black Acting Methods*. Oxford: Routledge.

Lugering, M. (2013) *The Expressive Actor*. Oxford: Routledge.

Mamet, D. (1998) *True and False*. London: Faber & Faber Ltd.

Meisner, S. and Longwell, D. (1987) *Sanford Meisner on Acting*. New York: Vintage Books.

Merlin, B. (2001) *Beyond Stanislavsky: The Psycho-physical Approach to Actor Training*. Oxford: Routledge.

Merlin, B. (2007) *The Complete Stanislavski Toolkit*. London: Nick Hern Books.

Merlin, B. (2010) *Acting the Basics*. Oxford: Routledge.

Oida, Y. and Marshal, L. (1997) *The Invisible Actor*. London: Methuen Drama.

Persley, N. H. and Ndounou, M. W. (2021) *Breaking It Down: Audition Techniques for Actors of the Global Majority*. London: Rowman & Littlefield Publishers.

Rea, K. (2015) *The Outstanding Actor: Seven Keys to Success*. London: Bloomsbury, Methuen Drama.

Watt-Smith, T. (2016) *The Book of Human Emotions: An Encyclopedia of Feeling from Anger to Wanderlust*. London: Wellcome Collection.

Wright, J. (2006) *Why Is That So Funny?* London: Nick Hern Books.

Movement

Bogart, A. and Landau, T. (2014) *The Viewpoints Book: A Practical Guide to Viewpoints and Composition*. London: Nick Hern Books.

Craig, M. (2017) *Biomechanics and Meyerhold*. Moscow: Russia Knowledge.

Dale, C. (2009) *The Subtle Body: An Encyclopedia of Your Energetic Anatomy*. London: Sounds True.

Donnellan, D. (2005) *The Actor and the Target*. London: Nick Hern Books.

Ewan, V. and Green, D. (2014) *Actor Movement: Expression of the Physical Being*. London: Bloomsbury Methuen Drama.

Ewan, V. and Sagovsky, K. (2017) *Laban's Efforts in Action: A Movement Handbook for Actors with Online Video*. London: Bloomsbury.

Hall, E. (1988) *The Hidden Dimension*. New York: Bantam Doubleday Dell Publishing Group.

Kogler, C. R. (2018) *Stagecraft Fundamentals: A Guide and Reference for Theatrical Production*. Oxford: Routledge.

Lecoq, J. (2000) *The Moving Body (Le Corps Poétique): Teaching Creative Theatre*. Oxford: Routledge.

Marshall, L. (2008) *The Body Speaks: Performance and Physical Expression*. London: Methuen Drama.

Olsen, A. (1998) *Body Stories: A Guide to Experiential Anatomy*. Middletown, CT: Wesleyan University Press.

Suzuki, T. (2015) *Culture Is the Body*. New York: Theatre Communications Group.

Yakim, M. (1996) *Creating a Character: A Physical Approach to Acting*. New York: Applause; Reprint edition.

National Theatre – Frantic Assembly Masterclass: Learning to Fly: https://www.youtube.com/watch?v=Q4mXhW7TXQ8&list=-PLJgBmjHpqgs4s6c0MrG-pniFOTtvKncpG (Accessed 1 September 2023).

National Theatre – Movement Direction: Creating Character: https://www.youtube.com/watch?v=1RRc4tq2kpE&list=PLJgBmjHpqgs4s6c0MrG-pniFOTtvKncpG&index=5 (Accessed 1 September 2023).

TED Global 2012 – Amy Cuddy: Body Language and Power Poses: https://www.ted.com/talks/amy_cuddy_your_body_language_may_ shape_who_you_are (Accessed 1 September 2023).

Voice

Berry, C. (2000) *The Actor and the Text*. London: Virgin Books.

Berry, C. (2000) *Voice and the Actor*. London: Virgin Books.

Boston, J. and Cook, R. (2009) *Breath in Action: The Art of Breath in Vocal and Holistic Practice*. London: Jessica Kingsley Publishers.

Caban, A., Foh, J. and Parker, J. (2021) *Experiencing Speech: A Skills-Based, Panlingual Approach to Actor Training – A Beginner's Guide to Knight-Thompson Speechwork*. Oxford: Routledge.

Carey, D. and Clark Carey, R. (2010) *Verbal Arts Workbook*. London: Methuen Drama.

Elmes, S. (2005) *Talking for Britain: A Journey through the Nation's Dialects*. London: Penguin.

Gutenkunst, C. (2014) *Voice into Acting*. London: Methuen Drama.

Hammet, J. and Williams-Burrell, L. (2024) *The Accent Handbook*. London: Methuen Drama.

Houseman, B. (2008) *Tackling Text [and subtext]*. London: Nick Hern Books.

Houseman, B. (2002) *Finding Your Voice*. London: Nick Hern Books.

Jones, D. (1987) *An Outline of English Phonetics*. Stuttgart: Ernst Klett Verlag GmbH.

Kachru, B. (2005) *Asian Englishes: Beyond the Canon*. Hong Kong: Hong Kong University Press.

Kayes, G. (2004) *Singing and the Actor*. Oxford: Oxford University Press.

Linklater, K. and Slob, A. (2007) *Freeing the Natural Voice: Imagery and Art in the Practice of Voice and Language*. Hollywood: Drama Publishers/Quite Specific Media.

McGuire, B. (2016) *African Accents: A Workbook for Actors*. Oxford: Routledge.

Morrison, M. (2001) *Clear Speech*. London: A & C Black.

Nelson, J. (2017) *The Voice Exercise Book*. London: Nick Hern Books.

Rodenburg, P. (1982) *The Right to Speak*. London: Methuen.

Rodenburg, P. (1994) *The Need for Words*. London: Methuen.

Rodenburg, P. (2019) *The Actor Speaks*. 2nd revised edition. London: Methuen.

Sharpe, E. and Rowles, H. (2009) *How to Do Accents*. London: Oberon Books.

British Library – British Accents and Dialects:

https://www.bl.uk/british-accents-and-dialects (Accessed 1 September 2023).
International Dialects of English Archive – General American: https://www.dialectsarchive.com/general-american (Accessed 1 September 2023).
Pronunciation Studio – MLE: https://pronunciationstudio.com/mle-multicultural-london-english-accent/ (Accessed 1 September 2023).
What Is African American Vernacular English (AAVE)? https://www.thoughtco.com/african-american-vernacular-english-aave-1689045 (Accessed 1 September 2023).
An Introduction to Punctuation by Richard Nordquist: https://www.thoughtco.com/punctuation-definition-1691702 (Accessed 1 September).

Actors on acting

Callow, S. (2004) *Being an Actor*. New York: Vintage Books.
Sher, A. (2004) *Year of the King: An Actor's Diary*. London: Nick Hern Books.
Zucker, C. (2018) *Focus of Don't Think. Be. 20 Actors Talk about Training, Technique and Process*.
10 Actors on Acting https://www.youtube.com/watch?v=QIgtVngQQ9A (Accessed 1 September).
Conversations on Broadway – Chukwudi Iwuji Career Retrospective: https://www.youtube.com/watch?v=CMoXvp_buTQ (Accessed 1 September).
Kwame Kwei-Armah, BBC Sounds, Behind the Scenes, 10 October 2018: https://www.bbc.co.uk/sounds/play/m0000ndr (Accessed 26 August 2023).
WhatsOnStage – Indhu Interviews: Noma Dumezweni and Lucian Msamati: https://www.youtube.com/watch?time_continue=26&v=iNR4xty97cw&feature=emb_title (Accessed 1 September 2023).

History, genre and style

Allain, P. (2003) *The Art of Stillness: The Theatre Practice of Tadashi Suzuki*. London: Griffin.
Berry, J. (1991) *West African Folktales*. Evanston, IL: Northwestern University Press.

Biggin, R. (2017) *Immersive Theatre and Audience Experience: Space, Game and Story in the Work of Punchdrunk*. London: Palgrave Macmillan.
Boal, A. (2002) *Games for Actors and Non-Actors*. Oxford: Routledge.
Boal, A. (2008) *Theatre of the Oppressed*. London: Pluto Press.
Brewer, M. et al. (2014) *Modern and Contemporary Black British Drama*. Basingstoke: Palgrave Macmillan.
Brook, P. (1968) *The Empty Space*. London: Penguin.
Esslin, M. (2014) *The Theatre of the Absurd*. London: Bloomsbury Academic.
Eyre, R. and Wright, N. (2001) *Changing Stages: A View of British Theatre in the Twentieth Century*. London: Bloomsbury Publishing.
Freeman, J. (2019) *Approaches to Actor Training: International Perspectives*. London: Methuen.
Graham, S. and Hoggett, S. (2009) *Frantic Assembly Book of Devising*. Oxford: Routledge.
Hammond, W. and Steward, D. (2008) *Verbatim Verbatim: Techniques in Contemporary Documentary Theatre*. London: Oberon Books.
Herrington, J. (1998) *Ain't Sorry for Nothin' I Done: August Wilson's Process of Playwrights*. New York: Limelight Editions.
Mackintosh, I. (2003) *Architecture, Actor and Audience*. Oxford: Routledge.
Mitchel, K. (2009) *The Director's Craft: A Handbook for the Theatre*. Oxford: Routledge.
Salz, J. (2016) *A History of Japanese Theatre*. Cambridge: Cambridge University Press.
Truby, J. (2008) *The Anatomy of Story*. New York: Faber & Faber, Inc.
Unwin, S. (2014) *The Complete Brecht Toolkit*. London: Nick Hern Books.
Yoo, J. (2017) *A Korean Approach to Actor Training*. Oxford: Routledge.
Zarrilli, P. (2010) *Theatre Histories: An Introduction*. 2nd edition. Oxford: Routledge.
Company '1927' – 'The Animals and Children Took to the Streets': https://www.youtube.com/watch?v=syCH3VZwbeI (Accessed 1 September 2023).
The Enigma of Ivan Van Hove: https://www.youtube.com/watch?v=CHf8rKFRPFg (Accessed 1 September 2023).
Punchdrunk's *The Burnt City in London* – Opening Night: https://www.youtube.com/watch?v=Wnm_rUTib54 (Accessed 1 September 2023).

Shakespeare

Asbury, N. (2009) *Exit Pursued by a Badger: An Actor's Journey through History with Shakespeare*. London: Oberon Books.

Barton, J. (2009) *Playing Shakespeare*. London: Methuen Drama.

Linklater, K. (1992) *Freeing Shakespeare's Voice*. New York: Theatre Communication Group.

Rodenburg, P. (2002) *Speaking Shakespeare*. London: Methuen.

Sher, A. and Doran, A. (2007) *Woza Shakespeare: 'Titus Andronicus' in South Africa*. London: Methuen Drama.

Thompson, A. (2013) *Passing Strange: Shakespeare, Race, and Contemporary America*. Oxford: Oxford University Press.

Akala: Shakespeare Sonnet 18 (different versions to different beats): https://www.youtube.com/watch?v=_31_UDs7Iac (Accessed 1 September 2023).

Ben Crystal: Shakespeare, Sonnets, & Heart: https://www.youtube.com/watch?v=zaUvZTqLHrQ (Accessed 1 September 2023).

Hip-Hop & Shakespeare? – Akala at TEDxAldeburgh: https://www.youtube.com/watch?v=DSbtkLA3GrY (Accessed 1 September 2023).

Bashy – Hip-Hop Shakespeare: Richard II – 'Prison Speech': https://www.youtube.com/watch?v=WUwPvr6glVE&feature=youtu.be (Accessed 1 September 2023).

Jamal Ajala for Graeae Theatre: 'To be, or not to be …' Hamlet, in BSL: https://www.youtube.com/watch?v=DCIeSZQ_Gtc (Accessed 1 September 2023).

Judi Dench on Speaking Shakespeare and Verse lines: https://www.youtube.com/watch?v=cqIbbRWivfM (Accessed 1 September 2023).

Mark Rylance – Why you should hear and not see Shakespeare: https://www.theguardian.com/stage/video/2014/nov/14/mark-rylance-shakespeare-olivier-dench-rsc-video (Accessed 1 September 2023).

Maxine Peake 'To be or not to be' (2015): https://embed.theguardian.com/embed/video/stage/video/2015/mar/09/maxine-peake-as-hamlet-to-be-or-not-to-be-video (Accessed 1 September 2023).

Paapa Essiedu 'To be or not to be' (2018): https://www.youtube.com/watch?v=7dZMJM-LGzQ (Accessed 1 September 2023).

Shakespeare Solos (*Guardian Culture* – including Zawe Ashton, Riz Ahmed, Paterson Joseph, Eileen Atkins …): https://www.youtube.com/playlist?list=PLlfYT-Za_x2JuweuLmpYfi1AXhUNKz32g (Accessed 1 September 2023).

Muse of Fire interviews on Shakespeare – Tom Hiddleston, Ian McKellen, Judi Dench: https://www.youtube.com/watch?v=7JsrC8YQ-FU (Accessed 1 September 2023).

Theatre, film and audio context

Barr, T. (1997) *Acting for the Camera*. New York: William Morrow.

Britten B. (2014) *From Stage to Screen: A Theatre Actor's Guide to Working on Screen*. London: Bloomsbury Methuen Drama.

Churcher, M. (2003) *Acting for Film*. London: Virgin Books.

Swain, J. H. (2017*) The Science and Art of Acting for the Camera: A Practical Approach to Film, Television, and Commercial Acting*. London: Routledge.

Creating Gollum: https://www.youtube.com/watch?v=w_Z7YUyCEGE (Accessed 1 September 2023).

Wellbeing and Resilience in the Creative Industries

Cameron, J. (2021) *The Listening Path: The Creative Art of Attention – A Six Week Artist's Way Programme*. London: Souvenir Press.

Cameron, J. (2011) *The Artist's Way: A Course in Discovering and Recovering Your Creative Self*. New York: Jeremy P. Tarcher.

Coutu, D. L. and Edgar, H. (2002) Schein: The Anxiety of Learning, *Harvard Business Review*, 80(3): 100–6.

Ericcson, A. and Pool, R. (2017) *Peak: For Fans of Atomic Habits*. 1st edition. New York: Vintage.

Haig, M. (2021) *The Comfort Book*. London: Canongate.

Howard-Jones, P. (2018) *Evolution of the Learning Brain*. Oxford: Routledge.

Kushner, M. (2023) *How to Be a Multi-Hyphenate in the Theatre Business: Conversations, Advice, and Tips from 'Dear Multi-Hyphenate'*. Waltham, MA: Focal Press.

Robinson, K. (2021) *Out of Our Minds: The Power of Being Creative*. Minnesota, MN: Capstone.

Walter, D. (2020) *The Power of Discipline: How to Use Self Control and Mental Toughness to Achieve Your Goals*. Vancouver: Pristine Publishing.

TED – Brené Brown: The Power of Vulnerability: https://www.youtube.com/watch?v=iCvmsMzlF7o (Accessed 1 September 2023).

TEDx – Amma Asante: The Power of Defining Yourself: https://www.youtube.com/watch?v=lXNE4MD2X2w (Accessed 1 September 2023).

TEDx – Chris Bailey: How to Get Your Brain to Focus: https://www.youtube.com/watch?v=Hu4Yvq-g7_Y (Accessed 1 September 2023).

INDEX